TABLE OF CONTENTS

BREAKFASTS

BREAKFAST MEATLOAF

Preparation time: 18 minutes
Cooking time: 7 hours
Serving: 8
Ingredients:

- 12 oz. ground beef
- 1 teaspoon salt
- 1 teaspoon ground coriander
- 1 tablespoon ground mustard
- ¼ teaspoon ground chili pepper
- 6 oz. white bread
- ½ cup milk
- 1 teaspoon ground black pepper

- 3 tablespoon tomato sauce

Directions:

- Chop the white bread and combine it with the milk.
- Stir then set aside for 3 minutes.
- Meanwhile, combine the ground beef, salt, ground coriander, ground mustard, ground chili pepper, and ground black pepper.
- Stir the white bread mixture carefully and add it to the ground beef. Cover the bottom of the slow cooker bowl with foil.
- Shape the meatloaf and place the uncooked meatloaf in the slow cooker then spread it with the tomato sauce.
- Close the slow cooker lid and cook the meatloaf for 7 hours on LOW.
- Slice the prepared meatloaf and serve. Enjoy!

Nutrition:

- Calories - 214
- Fat - 14
- Carbs - 12.09
- Protein - 9

CARROT EGG BAKE

Preparation time: 10 minutes
Cooking time: 2 hours
Serving: 2
Ingredients:

- 1 carrot, grated
- 1 tablespoon coconut flour
- 3 eggs, beaten
- ½ teaspoon vanilla extract
- ¾ teaspoon ground cinnamon
- 1 tablespoon stevia extract
- 1 teaspoon butter
- ¾ cup heavy cream

Directions:

- Whisk together eggs with heavy cream, butter, vanilla extract, ground cinnamon, and stevia extract.
- When the liquid is smooth, add grated carrot and stir it with the help of the spoon.
- Pour the mixture in the crockpot and flatten the grated carrot to get the thin layer inside the egg liquid.
- Close the lid and cook egg Bake for 2 hours on High.

Nutrition:

- Calories - 314
- Fat - 26.1

- Carbs - 9.6
- Protein - 10.5

HONEY GRANOLA AND BLUEBERRY YOGURT

Serving: 4-8
Ingredients:

- 8 cups milk
- ½ cup yogurt starter or live yogurt
- Honey Granola
- Blueberries
- Honey

Directions:

- Set the slow cooker to LOW.
- Pour in milk.
- Cook on LOW for 2 ½ hours. Add 15 minutes to cooking if slow cooker is bigger than 2 quarts.
- Unplug after 2 ½ hours the cooker. Leave the pot covered and allow the milk to cool down for 3 hours.
- After the 3 hours, put ½ cup of the warmed milk in a small bowl. Add the yogurt starter or live yogurt and mix well.
- Pour back into the crock and stir.
- Replace the lid. Wrap the pot with a couple of thick towels or with a blanket
- Allow to stand for 8-12 hours.
- For thick yogurt, pour into a colander lined with cheese cloth. Strain until desired thickness is achieved.
- Straining Serving: about 1quart.
- Stir. Place in the refrigerator. It will keep up to a week.
- Serve chilled sweetened with honey and topped with ¼ cup of blueberries and of granola for each cup of yogurt.

Nutrition:

- Calories - 120
- Fat - 3 g
- Carbs - 21 g
- Protein - 2 g

CAULIFLOWER BREAKFAST PUDDING

Preparation time: 8-10 minutes
Cooking time: 20 minutes
Serving: 3-4
Ingredients:

- 1 cup cauliflower rice

- 2 teaspoons (finely ground cinnamon powder
- 1 ½ cups unsweetened coconut or almond milk
- 1 cup water
- 1 teaspoon pure vanilla extract
- Pinch of salt

Directions:

- Take an Instant Pot; open the top lid.
- Add all the ingredients in the cooking pot. Using a spatula, gently stir to combine well.
- Close the top lid and make sure the valve is sealed.
- Press "MANUAL" cooking function. Adjust cooking time to 20 minutes.
- Allow pressure to build and cook the ingredients for the set time.
- After the set cooking time ends, press "CANCEL" and then press "NPR". Instant Pot will slowly and naturally release the pressure for 8-10 minutes.
- Open the top lid, add the cooked mixture in serving plates.
- Serve warm.

Nutrition:

- Calories - 223
- Fat - 21g
- Carbs - 6.5g
- Protein - 3g

SPINACH AVOCADO BREAKFAST CHICKEN

Preparation time: 8-10 minutes
Cooking time: 20 minutes
Serving: 3
Ingredients:

- 1 large leek, finely chopped
- 1 cup avocado chunks
- 1 small onion, finely chopped
- 7 ounce boneless and skinless chicken breast, make bite-sized pieces
- 1 cup fresh spinach, chopped
- 3 tablespoons butter
- 1 teaspoon salt
- 1 garlic clove, crushed
- 1 cup cottage cheese
- ½ teaspoon dried rosemary

Directions:

- Take your Instant Pot; open the top lid. Plug it and turn it on.
- Press "SAUTe" setting and the pot will start heating up.
- In the cooking pot area, add the butter, salt, and meat. Stir and cook for 12-15 minutes until evenly brown from all sides.
- Add the avocado and continue to cook for 5 minutes. If needed, add more butter.
- Add the onions, garlic, and chopped leeks. Give it a good stir and cook to soften.

- Add the spinach and sprinkle with rosemary.
- Press "Cancel" button. Let it sit for 10 minutes and add the cooked recipe mix in serving plates.
- Stir in the cottage cheese and serve immediately.

Nutrition:

- Calories - 362
- Fat - 24g
- Carbs - 9g
- Protein - 31g

BREAKFAST CINNAMON BARS

Preparation + Cooking time: 25 minutes
Serving: 2
Ingredients:

- 2 tbsp coconut oil
- 1 cup unsweetened almond milk
- 2 large eggs
- 1/3 cup hemp seeds
- 1 tbsp almonds, chopped
- 1/3 cup pumpkin puree
- 2 tbsp sesame seeds
- Spices: 2 tbsp swerve

Directions:

- Line a small baking dish with some parchment paper.
- Set aside.
- Place coconut oil and swerve in a microwave-safe bowl and microwave for 1 minute. Whisk together and Plug in the instant pot and pour in 1 cup of water in the inner pot. Position the trivet and place the baking dish on top.
- Seal the lid and set the steam release handle to the "Sealing" position. Press the "MANUAL" button and set the timer for 15 minutes on high pressure.
- When done, perform a quick pressure release by moving the pressure valve to the "Venting" position.
- Carefully open the lid and remove the dish.
- Chill for a while and cut into 4 bars.
- Serve immediately.
- Calories - 417
- Fat - 36.7g
- Carbs - 5g
- Protein - 17g

COCOA CHERRY BOWLS

Preparation time: 5 minutes
Cooking time: 3 hours
Serving: 4

Ingredients:

- 3 cups almond milk
- 2 tablespoons ground flaxseeds
- 2 tablespoons cocoa powder
- 1/3 cup cherries, pitted
- 3 tablespoons coconut sugar
- ½ teaspoon vanilla extract

Directions:

- In your slow cooker, mix all the ingredients, cover and cook on high for 3 hours.
- Divide everything into bowls and serve for breakfast.

Nutrition:

- Calories - 461
- Fat - 44,4
- Carbs - 23
- Protein - 5,3

JAMAICAN CORNMEAL PORRIDGE

Serving: 4
Preparation time: 5 minutes
Cooking time: 20 minutes
Ingredients:

- 4 cups water, divided
- 1 cup yellow cornmeal
- 1 cup milk
- 2 sticks of cinnamon
- 3 pimento berries
- 1 teaspoon vanilla extract
- ½ teaspoon nutmeg, ground
- ½ cup sweetened condensed milk

Directions:

- In a bowl, combine half of the water and cornmeal. Set aside.
- Press the Porridge button on the Instant Pot.
- Add the remaining water and milk into the Instant Pot. Stir in the cinnamon, pimento berries, vanilla extract, and nutmeg.
- Pour in the cornmeal mixture then stir.
- Close the lid and adjust the cooking time to 6 minutes.
- Do natural pressure release.
- Drizzle with condensed milk on top.

Nutrition:

- Calories - 241

- Carbs - 35.8g
- Protein - 5.6g
- Fat - 3.8g

CLASSIC APPLE OATS

Preparation time: 5 minutes
Cooking time: 5 minutes
Serving: 2
Ingredients:

- ½ teaspoon cinnamon
- ¼ teaspoon ginger
- 2 apples, make half-inch chunks
- ½ cup oats, steel cut
- 1 ½ cups water
- Maple syrup, as needed
- Pinch of salt
- Pinch of clove
- Pinch of nutmeg

Directions:

- Take Instant Pot and carefully arrange it over a clean, dry kitchen platform. Turn on the appliance.
- In the cooking pot area, add the water, oats, cinnamon, ginger, clove, nutmeg, apple and salt. Stir the ingredients gently.
- Close the pot lid and seal the valve to avoid any leakage. Find and press "MANUAL" cooking setting and set cooking time to 5 minutes.
- Allow the recipe ingredients to cook for the set time, and after that, the timer reads "zero".
- Press "Cancel" and press "NPR" setting for natural pressure release. It takes 8-10 times for all inside pressure to release.
- Open the pot and arrange the cooked recipe in serving plates.
- Sweeten as needed with maple or agave syrup and serve immediately. Top with some chopped nuts, optional.

Nutrition:

- Calories - 248
- Fat - 5.5g
- Carbs - 52g
- Protein - 7g

DELICIOUS CARROT BREAKFAST

Preparation time: 10 minutes
Cooking time: 6 hours
Serving: 10
Ingredients:

- 1 cup raisins
- 6 cups water
- 23 ounces applesauce, unsweetened
- 1/3 cup splenda
- 2 tablespoons cinnamon powder
- 14 ounces carrots, shredded
- 8 ounces canned pineapple, crushed
- 1 tablespoon pumpkin pie spice

Directions:

- In your slow cooker, mix carrots with applesauce, raisins, splenda, cinnamon, pineapple and pumpkin pie spice, stir, cover and cook on Low for 6 hours.
- Divide into bowls and serve for breakfast.
- Enjoy!

Nutrition:

- Calories - 139
- Fat - 2
- Carbs - 20
- Protein - 4

CHIA RUM PANCAKES

Preparation + Cooking time: 10 minutes
Serving: 3
Ingredients:

- 2 tbsp almond flour
- 4 large eggs, beaten
- 4 oz cream cheese, softened
- 1 tbsp erythritol
- 2 tbsp chia seeds
- 2 tbsp shredded coconut, unsweetened
- 1 tbsp butter, melted
- Spices: ¼ tsp salt
- ¼ tsp powdered stevia
- 1 tsp rum extract

Directions:

- In a large mixing bowl, combine all ingredients except coconut. Mix until smooth and creamy.
- Plug in your instant pot and grease the stainless steel insert with melted butter. Pour about 1/3 of the mixture in the pot and close the lid. Adjust the steam release handle and press the "MANUAL" button. Set the timer for 2 minutes and cook on "High" pressure.
- When you hear the cooker's end signal, perform a quick release of the pressure and open the pot. With a large kitchen spatula, remove the pancake from the pot.
- Repeat the process with the remaining batter.
- Sprinkle the pancakes with shredded coconut and serve immediately.

- Calories - 350
- Fat - 29.9g
- Carbs - 8g
- Protein - 14g

HEALTHY OATS AND QUINOA BREAKFAST

Serving: 6
Ingredients:

- Cooking spray
- 1 ½ cups of steel cut oats (don't replace with any other type of oats
- ½ cup quinoa (rinsed)
- 4 tablespoons brown sugar
- 2 tablespoons pure maple syrup
- 1 ½ teaspoons vanilla extract
- ¼ teaspoon salt
- 4 ½ cups of water
- Optional: fresh berries, extra sugar for topping

Directions:

- Coat the inside of the cooker with the cooking spray.
- Combine all the ingredients in the slow cooker and mix well.
- Cover and cook for 6 hours on LOW. (Cooking for longer than 6 hours may make it mushy.)
- After 6 hours turn off the heat and Serve immediately with desired toppings.

Nutrition:

- Calories - 343
- Fat - 9.8 g
- Carbs - 58.3 g
- Protein - 10.4 g

SAUSAGE BREAKFAST CASSEROLE

Preparation time: 10 minutes
Cooking time: 4 hours
Serving: 3
Ingredients:

- 6 oz sausages, chopped
- ½ teaspoon cayenne pepper
- ¾ cup of coconut milk
- 2 egg, whisked
- 3 oz Feta cheese, crumbled
- ¼ teaspoon ground black pepper
- 1 tablespoon fresh parsley, chopped
- 3 oz celery stalk, chopped

Directions:

- Place sausages in the crockpot.
- Then sprinkle them with ground black pepper, celery stalk, and fresh parsley.
- Add whisked eggs and coconut milk.
- Stir the ingredients gently and add crumbled cheese.
- Close the lid.
- Cook casserole for 4 hours on High.

Nutrition:

- Calories - 453
- Fat - 39.5
- Carbs - 5.9
- Protein - 20.4

ZUCCHINI OMELET

Preparation time: 4 minutes
Cooking time: 3 hours and 30 minutes
Serving: 6
Ingredients:

- 1½ cups red onion, chopped
- 1 tablespoon olive oil
- 2 garlic cloves, minced
- 2 teaspoons fresh basil, chopped
- 6 eggs, whisked
- A pinch of sea salt and black pepper
- 8 cups zucchini, sliced
- 6 ounces fresh tomatoes, peeled, crushed

Directions:

- In a bowl, mix all the ingredients except the oil and the basil.
- Grease the slow cooker with the oil, spread the omelet mix in the bowl, cover and cook on low for 3 hours and 30 minutes.
- Divide the omelet between plates, sprinkle the basil on top and serve for breakfast.

Nutrition:

- Calories - 156
- Fat - 7,2
- Carbs - 16,7
- Protein - 8,8

MONKEY BREAD

Preparation time: 20 minutes
Cooking time: 2 hours
Serving: 6

Ingredients:

- 12 oz. biscuit rolls
- 1 tablespoon ground cinnamon
- 3 oz. white sugar
- 1 teaspoon vanilla extract
- 4 tablespoon butter
- 1 egg white
- 4 tablespoon brown sugar

Directions:

- Cut the biscuit rolls into the small cubes.
- Then put the ground cinnamon and white sugar in the bowl. Stir the mixture with the help of the form gently. After this, melt the butter in the microwave oven.
- Add the ground cinnamon mixture in the melted butter and whisk till sugar is dissolved.
- After this, separate the biscuit roll cubes into 2 parts and place the first part in the slow cooker vessel.
- Then sprinkle the layer of the biscuit cubes with the melted butter mixture and add the second part of the biscuit rolls.
- Close the slow cooker lid and cook the dish for 2 hours on HIGH. Meanwhile, whisk the egg white till the strong peaks and add the brown sugar. Continue to whisk the egg white for 1 minute more - the icing is cooked.
- When the monkey bread is done - remove it from the slow cooker and chill well.
- Spread the surface of the monkey bread with the icing. Enjoy!

Nutrition:

- Calories - 313
- Fat - 16.8
- Carbs - 34.14
- Protein - 7

HEALTHY BREAKFAST CASSEROLE

Serving: 4
Ingredients:

- 1 cup tofu
- ½ cup milk
- 1 tablespoon ground mustard
- ¼ teaspoon garlic salt
- ½ teaspoon salt
- ¼ teaspoon pepper
- 1 (15-ounce bag frozen hash browns
- ¼ onion, roughly chopped
- 1 bell pepper, roughly chopped
- ½ small head of broccoli, roughly chopped
- 6 ounces vegan cheddar cheese (optional)

Directions:

- In a blender, combine the tofu and milk, and puree until smooth.
- In a medium-sized bowl, whisk together the tofu puree, mustard, garlic salt, salt, and pepper. Set aside.
- Lightly grease the bottom of your slow cooker. Place half the hash browns on the bottom. Layer with chopped onion, bell peppers, broccoli, and vegan cheese (if using). Add the rest of the hash browns, then top with the rest of the onion, bell peppers, broccoli, and cheese. Pour the puree mixture on top.
- Cover the slow cooker and cook for 4 hours on LOW. After 4 hours, turn off the slow cooker, and remove the lid carefully.
- Serve hot!

Nutrition:

- Calories - 220
- Fat - 11.2 g
- Carbs - 19.5 g
- Protein - 22.1 g

BOILED EGGS WITH SPINACH

Preparation + Cooking time: 25 minutes
Serving: 2
Ingredients:

- 1 lb spinach, chopped
- 4 large eggs
- 1 tbsp olives
- 3 tbsp olive oil
- 1 tbsp butter
- Spices: 1 tbsp mustard seeds
- 1 tbsp raw almonds
- ½ tsp chili flakes
- ½ tsp sea salt

Directions:

- Rinse the spinach thoroughly under cold running water and drain in a large colander.
- Set aside.
- Plug in the instant pot and pour in three cups of water in the stainless steel insert. Add eggs and close the lid. Adjust the steam release handle and press the "MANUAL" button. Set the timer for 4 minutes and cook on high pressure.
- When done, press the "Cancel" button and perform a quick pressure release by
- moving the pressure valve to the "Venting" position. Carefully, open the lid and Clean and pat dry the insert with a kitchen towel and place in the pot. Grease with some olive oil and press the "Saute" button.
- Add spinach and cook for 2-3 minutes, stirring occasionally.
- Now, stir in one tablespoon of butter and season with salt and chili flakes.
- Mix well and cook for one minute.
- Turn off the pot and sprinkle with nuts.
- Gently peel and slice each egg in half, lengthwise. Optionally, serve with sliced avocado and drizzle with some more olive oil.

- Calories - 414
- Fat - 36.8g
- Carbs - 4.1g
- Protein - 17.7g

HOLLANDAISE EGGS AND HAM

Preparation + Cooking time: 10 minutes
Serving: 2
Ingredients:

- 2 Eggs
- 2 tbsp. Hollandaise Sauce
- 2 Ham Slices, chopped
- 1 ½ cups plus 2 tbsp. Water

Directions:

- Pour 1 ½ cups water into your IP and lower the rack.
- Crack the eggs into 2 ramekins. Make sure to keep the yolks intact.
- Add a tablespoon of water on top.
- Place the ramekins in the IP and close the lid.
- Cook on STEAM for 2-3 minutes.
- Top with chopped ham and Hollandaise sauce.
- Serve and enjoy!
- Calories - 271
- Fat - 16.2g
- Carbs - 5.2g
- Protein - 25.3g

AROMATIC PEAR JAM

Serving: 10
Ingredients:

- 3 cups pears, peeled and chopped
- ½ teaspoon culinary lavender
- ½ teaspoon rose water
- Sweetener of your choice (as per taste

Directions:

- Place the pears and lavender into the slow cooker.
- Cover and cook for 7-8 hours, stirring occasionally.
- Add rosewater, and sweeten to taste.

Nutrition:

- Calories - 132
- Fat - 0 g
- Carbs - 34 g

- Protein - 0 g

VEGETABLES AND VEGETERIAN

ITALIAN ZUCCHINI

Serving: 4
Ingredients:

- 1 1/4 lb zucchini, sliced
- 1/4 cup chopped green bell pepper
- 1/4 cup chopped onion
- 3 oz unsalted tomato paste
- 2 oz sliced mushrooms
- 4 Tbsp unsalted butter
- 1 Tbsp Italian seasoning
- 2 oz shredded mozzarella cheese
- 1/2 cup water

Directions:

- Melt the butter over medium flame in a saucepan. Saute the green pepper and onion until tender. Scrape mixture into the slow cooker.
- Add the mushrooms, water, tomato paste, and Italian seasoning in the slow cooker. Gently stir in the zucchini.
- Cover and cook for 8 hours on low.

Nutrition:

- Calories - 145

TOMATO BASIL RISOTTO

Serving: 6
Ingredients:

- 1 cup Arborio rice
- 1 cup white wine, dry
- 3 cups vegetable broth
- ¼ cup fresh basil
- 3 cloves garlic
- 3 tomatoes, medium, diced
- 1 tablespoon vegan butter
- Salt and pepper
- Optional: Vegan Parmesan

Directions:

- Add all ingredients, except for the basil and butter, to the slow cooker.

- Cook on high for 2 hours, or until all liquid has absorbed and rice is tender. Add more liquid as needed.
- When the rice has finished cooking, add the butter and basil. Mix together and serve warm.

Nutrition:

- Calories - 471
- Fat - 3 g
- Carbs - 92 g
- Protein - 9 g

SAVOY CABBAGE BAKE

Preparation time: 15 minutes
Cooking time: 2.5 hours
Serving: 6
Ingredients:

- 1-pound savoy cabbage
- ½ cup of coconut milk
- 2 oz Parmesan, grated
- 1 tablespoon almond butter, softened
- 1 teaspoon ground paprika
- 1 teaspoon turmeric
- ½ teaspoon cayenne pepper
- 2 tablespoons almond flour

Directions:

- Shred the savoy cabbage and place it in the crockpot.
- In the bowl, combine together coconut milk, grated Parmesan, almond butter, ground paprika, turmeric, cayenne pepper, and almond flour.
- Stir the liquid until homogenous.
- Then pour it over the savoy cabbage and close the lid.
- Cook the meal for 2.5 hours on High.

Nutrition:

- Calories - 168
- Fat - 13.2
- Carbs - 8.9
- Protein - 7.1

HORCHATA LATTE

Serving: 8
Ingredients:

- 1 cup rice (long grain white is the most authentic Mexican option; use brown rice for a nutty flavor

- 5 cups water, hot
- 2 tablespoons instant coffee
- 1 cup coconut milk
- 2 cinnamon sticks
- ..." cup maple syrup
- 1 teaspoon vanilla extract

Directions:

- Mix the hot water, cinnamon, and rice together. Allow to sit overnight or for at least 6 hours.
- Pour the water-and-rice mixture into the blender and blend until smooth. No need to remove the cinnamon. Strain through a cheesecloth into the slow cooker.
- Add the maple syrup, coffee, and vanilla. Cook on low for 4 hours.
- Serve warm, or over ice for a more authentic experience.

Nutrition:

- Calories - 181
- Fat - 6 g
- Carbs - 29 g
- Protein - 2 g

CREAMY ZUCCHINI SOUP

Preparation + Cooking time: 15 minutes
Serving: 4
Ingredients:

- 4 medium-sized zucchinis; peeled and chopped.
- 1 small onion; chopped
- 2 cups vegetable stock
- 2 garlic cloves; crushed
- 1 tablespoon butter
- 2 cups heavy cream
- 1/2 teaspoon dried oregano; ground.
- 1/2 teaspoon black pepper; ground.
- 1 teaspoon dried parsley; ground.
- 1 teaspoon sea salt

Directions:

- Plug in the instant pot and add butter to the stainless steel insert. Press the "SAUTE" button and melt, stirring gently with a wooden spatula.
- Add onions, garlic, and chopped zucchinis. Cook for 3 minutes, stirring occasionally.
- Pour in the vegetable broth and sprinkle with salt, oregano, pepper, and parsley. Stir well and lock the lid. Adjust the steam release handle and press the "MANUAL" button. Set the timer for 5 minutes and cook on "HIGH" pressure.
- When done, perform a quick release of the pressure by moving the valve to the "VENTING" position.
- Open the pot and

Nutrition:

- Calories - 277
- Fat - 25.5g
- Carbs - 8.1g
- Protein - 4.2g

BALSAMIC PORK WITH SHIITAKE AND BROCCOLI

Preparation + Cooking time: 50 minutes
Serving: 4
Ingredients:

- 2 lbs pork shoulder, boneless
- 2 cups broccoli, cut into florets
- 10 oz shiitake mushrooms, sliced
- 3 tbsp soy sauce
- 2 tbsp oyster sauce
- 3 tbsp balsamic vinegar
- 3 tbsp butter
- 2 cups beef broth
- Spices: 2 bay leaves
- 1 ½ tsp sea salt
- 2 tsp peppercorn

Directions:

- Rinse well the meat and place in the pot. Sprinkle with salt and peppercorn. Pour in the broth and one cup of water. Add bay leaves and seal the lid. Set the steam release handle and press the "MANUAL" button.
- Cook for 25 minutes on high pressure.
- When done, perform a quick pressure release and open the lid. Remove half of the remaining liquid and add broccoli, shiitake, soy sauce, oyster sauce, balsamic vinegar, and butter.
- Seal the lid again and continue to cook for another 8 minutes on the "MANUAL" mode.
- When done, release the pressure naturally and serve immediately.
- Calories - 483
- Fat - 17.6g
- Carbs - 11.7g
- Protein - 65g

AROMATIC ROSEMARY GARLIC POTATOES

Serving: 4
Cooking time: 2 minutes
Preparation time: 30 minutes
Ingredients:

- 1 pound potatoes, peeled and sliced thinly

- 2 garlic cloves
- ½ teaspoon salt
- 1 tablespoon olive oil
- 2 sprigs of rosemary

Directions:

- Place a trivet or steamer basket in the Instant Pot and pour in a cup of water.
- In a baking dish that can fit inside the Instant Pot, combine all ingredients and toss to coat everything.
- Cover the baking dish with aluminum foil and place on the steamer basket.
- Close the lid and press the Steam button.
- Adjust the cooking time to 30 minutes
- Do quick pressure release.

Nutrition:

- Calories - 119
- Carbs - 20.31g
- Protein - 2.39g
- Fat - 3.48g

SUN-DRIED TOMATO POLENTA

Serving: 8
Cooking time: 2 minutes
Preparation time: 10 minutes
Ingredients:

- 2 tablespoons olive oil
- 2 cloves of garlic, minced
- ½ cup onion, chopped
- 4 cups vegetable stock
- 1/3 cup sun-dried tomatoes, finely chopped
- 1 bay leaf
- 1 teaspoon salt
- 2 tablespoons parsley, chopped
- 2 teaspoons oregano, chopped
- 3 tablespoons basil, chopped
- 1 teaspoon rosemary, chopped
- 1 cup polenta

Directions:

- Press the Saute button on the Instant Pot and add the oil.
- Saute the garlic and onions for 3 minutes until fragrant.
- Add the stock, sun-dried tomatoes, bay leaf, salt, parsley, oregano, basil, and rosemary. Stir to combine.
- Sprinkle polenta on top but do not stir.
- Close the lid and adjust the cooking time to 5 minutes.
- Do natural pressure release.

Nutrition:

- Calories - 69
- Carbs - 8.48g
- Protein - 1.07g
- Fat - 3.61g

CREAMY BACON BROCCOLI

Preparation + Cooking time: 20 minutes
Serving: 3
Ingredients:

- 1-pound broccoli; chopped.
- 1/4 cup Greek yogurt; full-fat
- 1 tablespoon fresh parsley; finely chopped
- 1/4 cup cheddar cheese
- 5 large bacon slices; chopped.
- 1 tablespoon olive oil
- 1/2 teaspoon red chili flakes
- 1/2 teaspoon Italian seasoning
- 1/2 teaspoon garlic powder
- 1/2 teaspoon salt

Directions:

- Plug in your instant pot and press the "SAUTE" button. Add bacon and cook for 3 minutes, or until crisp. Remove from the pot and combine with Greek yogurt and cheddar cheese, Set aside
- Now; grease the stainless steel with olive oil. Add broccoli and cook for 4-5 minutes.
- Stir in the previously prepared Greek yogurt mixture and sprinkle with garlic powder, Italian seasoning, salt, and red chili flakes. Continue to cook for 5 more minutes, stirring occasionally.
- Turn off the pot and a
- serving dish
- Sprinkle with finely chopped parsley and serve immediately.

Nutrition:

- Calories - 318
- Fat - 22.1g
- Carbs - 7.8g
- Protein - 20.1g

ULTIMATE CHEESY CAULIFLOWER

Serving: 6
Ingredients:

- 3 cups cauliflower, sliced
- 4 cups fresh spinach, chopped

- ¼ cup butter, cubed
- 1 tablespoon shallots, diced
- 1 teaspoon salt
- 1 teaspoon black pepper
- ½ cup vegetable stock
- ¼ cup heavy cream
- 1 cup Gorgonzola cheese, crumbled
- 1 cup Swiss cheese, shredded
- 1 tablespoon fresh thyme

Directions:

- Place the cauliflower, spinach, butter, shallots, salt, black pepper, and vegetable stock in a slow cooker.
- Cover and cook on high for 4 hours.
- Add the heavy cream, Gorgonzola cheese, Swiss cheese, and thyme. Mix well.
- Cover and cook an additional 30-40 minutes before serving.

Nutrition:

- Calories - 266.1
- Fat - 22.5 g
- Carbs - 5.8 g
- Protein - 11.7 g

VEGETABLE MEXICAN STEW

Serving: 8
Ingredients:

- 5 cups chicken broth
- 1 head of cabbage, chopped
- 2 large
- 1 zucchini
- 1 large onion, chopped
- 2 jalapenos, chopped
- 1 green capsicum, chopped
- 4 tomatoes, chopped
- 5 cloves garlic
- 1 tablespoon chili powder
- 2 tablespoons tomato paste
- 1 tablespoon cu minutes
- ¼ cup olive oil
- 1 teaspoon black pepper
- 1 teaspoon salt
- ¼ cup sour cream
- Fresh cilantro, chopped.

Directions:

- To a crock pot over medium-high heat, add the olive oil, onion and garlic. Cook until golden brown.
- Add in the remaining ingredients and cook for 3-4 hours on low.

Nutrition:
Nutrition:

- Calories - 222
- Fat - 7 g
- Carbs - 8 g
- Protein - 37 g

ZUCCHINI RAGOUT

Serving: 4
Ingredients:

- 3 oz fresh spinach
- 1/3 cup diced red onion
- 2
- zucchini, diced
- 1 large carrot, peeled and diced
- 1 celery stalk, diced
- 2 Tbsp tomato paste
- 1 small parsnip, diced
- 3 Tbsp water
- 2/3 Tbsp minced fresh oregano
- 2/3 Tbsp minced fresh basil
- 2/3 Tbsp mince d fresh flat leaf parsley
- 1/6 tsp salt
- 2/3 tsp ground black pepper

Directions:

- Place the spinach, zucchini, red onion, celery, carrots, and parsnip into the slow cooker. Combine the water and tomato paste in a small bowl, then add the fresh herbs, salt and pepper. Stir everything into the slow cooker.
- Cover and cook for 2 hours on low. Before serving, stir well.

Nutrition:

- Calories - 60

SAVORY RANCH POTATOES

Preparation + Cooking time: 25 minutes
Serving: 2-4
Ingredients:

- 2 tbsp butter
- 3 large yellow potatoes, cubed

- 2 tbsp Ranch dressing or seasoning mix
- ½ cup water
- Salt and ground black pepper to taste

Directions:

- Preheat the Instant Pot by selecting Saute. Once hot, add the butter and melt it.
- Add the potatoes and stir well.
- Sprinkle with Ranch seasoning and stir. Add the water. Close and lock the lid.
- Press the CANCEL button to reset the cooking program, then press the MANUAL button and set the cooking time for 6 minutes at HIGH pressure.
- When the timer beeps, use a Quick Release
- Carefully unlock the lid.
- Season with salt and pepper and serve.

PROVINCIAL RATATOUILLE

Preparation + Cooking time: 26 minutes
Serving: 6
Ingredients:

- 1 sliced into thin circles large zucchini
- 1 sliced into thin circles medium eggplant
- 2 sliced into thin disks medium tomatoes
- 1 sliced into thin circles small yellow onion
- 1 tbsp. dried thyme (divided)
- Salt and freshly ground black pepper, to taste
- 2 finely chopped large garlic cloves
- 2 tbsp. olive oil
- 1 tbsp. apple cider vinegar
- 1 cup water

Directions:

- In a bowl, add all vegetables and sprinkle with half of the thyme, salt and black pepper.
- In the bottom of a foil lined round springform pan, spread some garlic.
- Layer the vegetables into a tight snail-like circle over garlic, alternating between eggplant, zucchini, onion and tomato slices. (Keep the slices close together, overlapping slightly).
- Sprinkle with the remaining garlic, thyme, salt and black pepper and drizzle with oil and vinegar.
- In the bottom of Instant Pot, arrange a steamer trivet and pour 1 cup of water.
- Place the pan on top of the trivet.
- Secure the lid and place the pressure valve to "Seal" position.
- Select "MANUAL" and cook under "Low Pressure" for about 6 minutes.
- Select the "Cancel" and carefully do a "Natural" release for about 6 minutes and then do a "Quick" release.

Nutrition:

- Calories - 86

- Fat - 5.1g
- Carbs - 1.7g
- Protein - 2.1g

KETO COLLARD GREENS TOFU

Preparation + Cooking time: 15 minutes
Serving: 2
Ingredients:

- 1-pound collard greens; chopped.
- 3 garlic cloves; finely chopped.
- 1/4 cup walnuts; roughly chopped.
- 1 cup vegetable stock
- 2 teaspoon olive oil
- 1 cup tofu; cut into small cubes
- 1 tablespoon butter
- 2 teaspoon balsamic vinegar
- 1/4 teaspoon black pepper; ground
- 1/4 teaspoon red chili flakes
- 1/2 teaspoon smoked paprika; ground
- 1/2 teaspoon sea salt

Directions:

- Plug in the instant pot and grease the stainless steel insert with olive oil. Press the "SAUTE" button and add garlic and tofu. Sprinkle with some salt and pepper and stir-fry for 2-3 minutes. Remove all to a plate and set aside.
- Now; add butter and stir with a wooden spatula until melts. Add collard greens and cook for 2-3 minutes, or until wilted. Sprinkle with smoked paprika, chili flakes, and a pinch of salt. Pour in the vegetable broth and lock the lid.
- Set the steam release handle and press the "MANUAL" button. Set the timer for 2 minutes and cook on "HIGH" pressure.
- When you hear the cooker's end signal, perform a quick release of the pressure and open the pot
- Stir in the balsamic vinegar and walnuts. a
- serving plate and top with tofu and garlic mixture. Serve and enjoy.

Nutrition:

- Calories - 351
- Fat - 26.6g
- Carbs - 8.3g
- Protein - 19.7g

BELL PEPPERS IN WARM SAUCE

Preparation + Cooking time: 20 minutes
Serving: 4
Ingredients:

- 1 medium-sized red bell pepper; chopped
- 1 medium-sized green bell pepper; chopped
- 1 medium-sized yellow bell pepper; chopped
- 1 small chili pepper; finely chopped.
- 1 medium-sized onion; sliced
- 1 small celery stalk; chopped
- 2 tablespoon olive oil
- 1 tablespoon butter
- 2 teaspoon balsamic vinegar
- 2 garlic cloves; finely chopped
- 1/2 cup tomatoes; diced
- 1/4 teaspoon dried thyme; ground.
- 1/2 teaspoon black pepper; ground.
- 1/4 teaspoon ginger powder
- 1/2 teaspoon salt

Directions:

- In a food processor, combine tomatoes, garlic, chili pepper, olive oil, balsamic vinegar, and all spices. Blend until smooth and creamy, Set aside.
- Plug in the instant pot and add butter to the stainless steel insert. Press the "SAUTE" button and melt.
- Add bell peppers and onions. Stir-fry for 3-4 minutes, or until the onions Add celery and pour in the previously blended mixture. Securely lock the lid and set the steam release handle. Press the "MANUAL" button and set the timer for 3 minutes. Cook on "HIGH" pressure
- When you hear the cooker's end signal, perform a quick pressure release by moving the valve to the "VENTING" position.
- Open the pot and a serving bowl. Optionally, top with some grated cheese such as parmesan or cheddar cheese.

Nutrition:

- Calories - 179
- Fat - 13.6g
- Carbs - 11.9g
- Protein - 2.2g

SWEET AND SPICY CARROTS

Preparation + Cooking time: 18 minutes
Serving: 4
Ingredients:

- 1 pound quartered lengthwise and halved carrots
- 1 tbsp. Erythritol
- 2 tbsp. butter
- 3 tsp ground mustard
- 1 tsp ground cu minutes
- ½ tsp cayenne pepper
- ¼ tsp red pepper flakes

- Salt and freshly ground black pepper, to taste
- 1/8 tsp ground cinnamon

Directions:

- In the bottom of Instant Pot, arrange a steamer basket and pour 1 cup of water.
- Place the carrots into the steamer basket.
- Secure the lid and place the pressure valve to "Seal" position.
- Select "MANUAL" and cook under "High Pressure" for about 1 minute.
- Select the "Cancel" and carefully do a "Quick" release.
- Remove the lid and Remove water from the pot and with paper towels, pat dry.
- Select the "Saute" mode for Power Pressure Cooker. In the pot of Pressure Cooker, melt butter and stir in the remaining ingredients.
- Stir in the carrots and cook for about 1 minute.
- Select the "Cancel" and serve warm with the sprinkling of cinnamon.

Nutrition:

- Calories - 112
- Fat - 6.6g
- Carbs - 3.50g
- Protein - 1.7g

MEDITERRANEAN STUFFED PEPPERS

Serving: 2
Ingredients:

- 2 large bell peppers
- ½ (15-ounce can cannellini beans, rinsed and drained
- ¼ cup couscous, cooked
- 2 scallions, white and green parts separated, thinly sliced
- 1 clove garlic, minced
- ½ teaspoon dried oregano
- Coarse salt and freshly ground pepper
- Lemon wedges, for serving

Directions:

- Cut a very thin layer off the base of each pepper so they sit flat. Slice the top, straight across under the stem, to make a cup. Discard the stems. Remove the ribs and seeds from the peppers.
- Add the beans, couscous, scallions (the white parts), garlic, and oregano to the bowl. Season with salt and pepper, and mix. Fill the peppers with the bean mixture, and place them in the slow cooker in a vertical position. Cover, and cook on HIGH for 4 hours.
- Sprinkle the peppers with the scallion greens, and serve with lemon slices.

Nutrition:

- Calories - 380
- Fat - 22.3 g
- Carbs - 27.3 g
- Protein - 17.2 g

SOUPS AND STEWS

WHOLE FOOD MINESTRONE SOUP

Serving: 6
Preparation time: 5 minutes
Cooking time: 10 minutes
Ingredients:

- 2 tablespoons olive oil
- 1 onion, diced
- 3 cloves of garlic, minced
- 2 stalks of celery, diced
- 1 carrot, diced
- 1 teaspoon dried basil
- 1 teaspoon dried oregano
- Salt and pepper to taste
- 1 can crushed tomatoes
- 1 can white cannellini beans, rinsed
- 1 bay leaf
- 4 cups bone broth
- 1 cup elbow pasta
- 1 cup kale leaves, chopped
- 1/3 cup parmesan cheese, grated

Directions:

- Press the Saute button on the Instant Pot.
- Heat the oil and saute the onions and garlic until fragrant.
- Stir in the celery, carrots, basil, and oregano. Season with salt and pepper to taste
- Add the tomatoes, beans, bay leaf. Pour in the bone broth.
- Stir in the elbow pasta.
- Close the lid and press the Manual button.
- Adjust the cooking time to 10 minutes.
- Do natural pressure release.
- Once the lid is open, add the kale leaves and parmesan cheese.

Nutrition:

- Calories - 143
- Carbs - 13.5g
- Protein - 6.4g
- Fat - 7.3g

PERFECT OXTAIL BROTH

Preparation + Cooking time: 1¾ hours
Serving: 8
Ingredients:

- 3¼ pounds oxtail
- 2 peeled and chopped medium carrots
- 2 chopped medium celery stalks
- 1 quartered medium skin-on yellow onion
- 1 parsley root
- 5 peeled garlic cloves
- 2 tbsp. fresh lemon juice
- 2-3 bay leaves
- Salt, to taste
- 8 cups filtered water

Directions:

- In the pot of Instant Pot, add all ingredients.
- Secure the lid and place the pressure valve to "Seal" position.
- Select "MANUAL" and cook under "High Pressure" for about 90 minutes.
- Select the "Cancel" and carefully do a "Natural" release.
- Remove the lid and through a fine mesh strainer, strain the broth.
- Keep aside at room temperature to cool completely.
- Remove solidified fat from the top of the chilled broth.
- You can preserve this broth in the refrigerator for about 5-7 days or up to 3-4 months in the freezer.

Nutrition:

- Calories - 333
- Fat - 18.6g
- Carbs - 0.45g
- Protein - 37.3g

BUFFALO CHICKEN SOUP

Preparation + Cooking time: 35 minutes
Serving: 4
Ingredients:

- 2 chicken breasts, boneless, skinless, frozen or fresh
- 1 clove garlic, chopped
- ¼ cup onion, diced
- ½ cup celery, diced
- 2 tbsp butter
- 1 tbsp ranch dressing mix
- 3 cups chicken broth
- 1/3 cup hot sauce
- 2 cups cheddar cheese, shredded
- 1 cup heavy cream

Directions:

- In the Instant Pot, combine the chicken breasts, garlic, onion, celery, butter, ranch dressing mix, broth, and hot sauce.
- Close and lock the lid. Select MANUAL and cook at HIGH pressure for 10 minutes.
- Once cooking is complete, let the pressure
- Release Naturally
- for 10 minutes.
- Release any remaining steam manually. Uncover the pot.
- Return to the pot.
- Add the cheese and heavy cream. Stir well. Let sit for 5 minutes and serve.

SPICY CHIPOTLE SHORT RIBS STEW

Preparation + Cooking time: 60 minutes
Serving: 6
Ingredients:

- For stew: 2 lbs beef short ribs
- 2 cups tomatoes, chopped
- 1 cup white onions, chopped
- 3 Poblano peppers, cut into strips
- 2 chipotle peppers, finely chopped
- 3 tbsp olive oil
- 3 cups beef broth
- Spices: 1 tsp salt
- ½ tsp white pepper, freshly ground

Directions:

- Rub the meat with salt and pepper.
- Set aside.
- Plug in the instant pot and grease the inner pot with olive oil. Press the "Saute" button and add peppers, tomatoes, and onions.
- Cook for 15 minutes, stirring occasionally.
- Now, pour in the broth and add the meat. Securely lock the lid and set the steam release handle to the "Sealing" position. Press the "MANUAL" button and set the timer for 35 minutes on high pressure.
- When you hear the end signal, perform a quick pressure release and open the lid.
- Serve warm.

Nutrition:

- Calories - 423
- Fat - 21.5g
- Carbs - 6.4g
- Protein - 47.6g

GERMAN LENTIL SOUP

Serving: 4

Ingredients:

- 1 cup dried brown lentils, rinsed, drained
- 1 bay leaf
- ½ cup chopped celery
- ½ cup chopped carrot
- ½ cup chopped onion
- ¼ tsp garlic powder
- 3 drops hot pepper sauce or to taste
- 1 ½ cups chicken stock
- ½ cup cooked, cubed ham
- 1/8 tsp freshly grated nutmeg
- 1/8 tsp caraway seeds
- ½ Tbsp chopped fresh parsley
- ½ tsp Worcestershire sauce
- ¼ tsp celery salt
- ¼ tsp pepper or to taste

Directions:

- Add brown lentils, bay leaf, celery, carrot, onion, garlic powder, hot pepper sauce, chicken stock, ham, nutmeg, caraway seeds, parsley, Worcestershire sauce, celery salt and pepper into the slow cooker.
- Stir well.
- Cover and cook for 8 hours on low or 4 hours on high. Stir occasionally. Add some water if desired.
- Taste and adjust the seasoning if required.
- Discard bay leaf after cooking.

Nutrition:

- Calories - 221

SAUSAGE BACON AND MUSHROOM CHOWDER

Preparation + Cooking time: 5-10 minutes
Serving: 14
Ingredients:

- 4 cups Chicken Broth
- 2 cups Heavy Cream
- 2 cups Mushrooms (sliced)
- 2 cups Ground Sausage (cooked)
- 6 rashers Bacon (fried and crumbled)
- 1 cup Daikon Radish (diced)
- ½ cup Onion (diced)
- ½ cup Red Bell Pepper (diced)
- ½ cup Parmesan Cheese
- 1 tbsp. Dried Parsley Leaves
- 1 tsp Garlic Powder
- 1 tsp Salt

- 1 tsp Ground Black Pepper
- ½ tsp Thyme

Directions:

- Place all ingredients in the Instant Pot.
- Place and lock the lid and manually set the cooking time to 5 minutes at high pressure.
- When done quick release the pressure.
- Serve warm.

Nutrition:

- Calories - 316
- Fat - 33g
- Carbs - 3g
- Protein - 14g

CAULIFLOWER SOUP

Preparation + Cooking time: 25 minutes
Serving: 4
Ingredients:

- 1 tbsp butter
- 1 large onion, chopped
- 3 cups chicken broth
- 1 medium cauliflower, chopped
- Salt and ground black pepper to taste

Directions:

- Preheat the Instant Pot by selecting SAUTe. Once hot, add the butter and melt it.
- Add the onion and saute for 4-5 minutes, until softened.
- Add the broth, cauliflower, salt and pepper. Stir well. Close and lock the lid.
- Press the CANCEL button to stop the SAUTE function, then select the MANUAL setting and set the cooking time for 5 minutes at HIGH pressure.
- Once timer goes off, use a
- Quick Release
- Carefully unlock the lid.
- With an immersion blender, blend the soup to your desired texture.
- Serve.

BEEF BORSCHT SOUP

Preparation + Cooking time: 40 minutes
Serving: 4-6
Ingredients:

- 2 lbs ground beef
- 3 beets, peeled and diced
- 2 large carrots, diced

- 3 stalks of celery, diced
- 1 onion, diced
- 2 cloves garlic, diced
- 3 cups shredded cabbage
- 6 cups beef stock
- ½ tbsp thyme
- 1 bay leaf
- Salt and ground black pepper to taste

Directions:

- Preheat the Instant Pot by selecting SAUTe.
- Add the ground beef and cook, stirring, for 5 minutes, until browned.
- Combine all the rest ingredients in the Instant Pot and stir to mix.
- Close and lock the lid.
- Press the CANCEL button to stop the SAUTE function, then select the MANUAL setting and set the cooking time for 15 minutes at HIGH pressure.
- Once timer goes off, allow to
- Naturally Release
- for 10 minutes, then release any remaining pressure manually.
- Uncover the pot.
- Let the dish sit for 5-10 minutes and serve.

GARLICKY CHICKEN BROTH

Preparation + Cooking time: 2¼ hours
Serving: 12
Ingredients:

- 1 (3-4-pound) grass-fed chicken bones
- 3 peeled and cut in half medium carrots
- 3 chopped celery ribs
- 1 medium quartered skin-on yellow onion
- 6 lightly smashed garlic cloves
- 1 bay leaf
- 8-10 peppercorns
- ½ cup mixed fresh herbs (sage, rosemary, thyme and or parsley)
- 1 tbsp. apple cider vinegar
- Salt, to taste
- Filtered water (as required)

Directions:

- In the pot of Instant Pot, add all ingredients with enough water to just cover the mixture.
- Secure the lid and place the pressure valve to "Seal" position.
- Select "MANUAL" and cook under "High Pressure" for about 120 minutes.
- Select the "Cancel" and carefully do a "Natural" release.
- Remove the lid and through a fine mesh strainer, strain the broth.
- Keep aside at room temperature to cool completely.
- Remove solidified fat from the top of the chilled broth.

- You can preserve this broth in the refrigerator for about 5-7 days or up to 3-4 months in the freezer.

Nutrition:

- Calories - 221
- Fat - 4.4g
- Carbs - 0.38g
- Protein - 38.8g

CALAMARI CAULIFLOWER STEW

Preparation + Cooking time: 40 minutes
Serving: 4
Ingredients:

- 1.5lbs calamari, cleaned and sliced
- 2 cups riced cauliflower
- 2 cups fish stock
- 1 cup collards
- 1 cup spinach
- 1 chopped onion.
- ½ cup white wine
- 2 tbsp. low sodium oyster sauce
- salt and pepper

Directions:

- Mix everything but the cauliflower, collards and spinach in your Instant Pot.
- Seal and cook on Meat 5 minutes.
- Depressurize naturally.
- Add the cauliflower and seal again.
- Cook on Stew 5 minutes.
- Depressurize naturally.
- Wilt the greens into it and serve.

Nutrition:

- Calories - 190
- Fat - 2g
- Carbs - 4g
- Protein - 38g

INSTANT POT CHEDDAR, BROCCOLI, AND POTATO SOUP

Serving: 6
Preparation time: 5 minutes
Cooking time: 7 minutes
Ingredients:

- 2 tablespoons butter
- 2 cloves of garlic, minced
- 1 broccoli head, cut into florets
- 2 pounds Yukon Gold potatoes, peeled and quartered
- 4 cups chicken broth
- Salt and pepper to taste
- 1 cup cheddar cheese, grated
- 6 slices of bacon, fried and crumbled

Directions:

- Press the Saute button on the Instant Pot.
- Heat the butter and saute the garlic until fragrant.
- Stir in the broccoli florets, potatoes, and chicken broth
- Season with salt and pepper to taste.
- Sprinkle with cheese on top.
- Close the lid and press the Soup button.
- Adjust the cooking time to 7 minutes.
- Do quick pressure release.
- Sprinkle with bacon bits on top.

Nutrition:

- Calories - 598
- Carbs - 34.4g
- Protein - 47.7g
- Fat - 29.5g

ITALIAN SAUSAGE STEW

Serving: 4
Preparation time: 5 minutes
Cooking time: 30 minutes
Ingredients:

- 2 tablespoons butter
- ½ pound ground pork
- ½ teaspoon onion powder
- ½ teaspoon garlic powder
- 1 ½ teaspoon basil
- ½ teaspoon thyme
- ¼ teaspoon cu minutes
- ½ teaspoon marjoram
- ¼ teaspoon cayenne
- 2 carrots, diced
- 2 stalks of celery, chopped
- ½ cup wine
- 1 can diced tomatoes
- 4 cups bone broth
- Salt and pepper
- A handful of kale, chopped

- ½ cup parmesan cheese, grated

Directions:

- Press the Saute button on the Instant Pot.
- Melt the oil and add the ground pork. Stir in the onion powder, garlic powder, basil, thyme, cumin, marjoram, and cayenne.
- Continue stirring the pork until lightly golden.
- Stir in the carrots, celery, wine, tomatoes, and bone broth.
- Season with salt and pepper.
- Close the lid and press the Manual button.
- Adjust the cooking time to 25 minutes.
- Do quick pressure release.
- Once the lid is open, press the Saute button and stir in the kale. Simmer until wilted.
- Sprinkle with parmesan cheese.

Nutrition:

- Calories - 304
- Carbs - 8.9g
- Protein - 21.3g
- Fat - 19.4 g

PAYNE STEW

Preparation + Cooking time: 60 minutes
Serving: 6
Ingredients:

- 1.5lbs boneless red meat
- 1 cup beef broth
- 2 onions
- 2 cups carrots
- 8 garlic cloves
- herbes de provence
- salt and pepper

Directions:

- Dice everything to the same rough size.
- Mix together in your Instant Pot.
- Cook on Stew for 55 minutes.
- Calories - 250
- Fat - 9g
- Carbs - 12g
- Protein - 31g

EASY LAMB STEW

Preparation + Cooking time: 45 minutes
Serving: 3

Ingredients:

- For stew: 1 lb lamb leg, chopped into bite-sized pieces
- 2 cups cabbage, shredded
- 6 garlic cloves, crushed
- 4 cups vegetable stock
- 2 tbsp butter, for serving
- Spices: 1 rosemary sprig
- 1 thyme sprig
- 1 bay leaf
- 1 tsp sea salt

Directions:

- Combine the ingredients in the pot and pour in the stock. Stir well and optionally season with some more salt or pepper.
- Seal the lid and set the steam release handle to the "Sealing" position. Press the "Meat" button and set the timer for 35 minutes.
- When you hear the end signal, press the "Cancel" button and release the pressure naturally.
- Using oven mitts, move the pressure valve to the "Venting" position to release any remaining pressure.
- Carefully open the lid and stir in butter. Let it sit for 2-3 minutes and serve immediately.

Nutrition:

- Calories - 378
- Fat - 19g
- Carbs - 3.9g
- Protein - 44.1g

LENTIL SOUP

Preparation + Cooking time: 35 minutes
Serving: 6
Ingredients:

- 2 tbsp olive oil
- 1 medium onion, chopped
- 3 cloves garlic, minced
- 2 carrots, sliced into ¼ inch pieces
- 1 lb red bliss or yukon gold potatoes
- 2 celery stalks, diced (optional
- 1½ tsp smoked paprika
- 1½ tsp cu minutes
- 1 cup red lentils, rinsed
- 1 cup green or brown lentils, rinsed
- 8 cups water
- 1 bunch rainbow chard or spinach, chopped
- Salt and ground black pepper to taste

Directions:

- Select the SAUTe setting on the Instant Pot and heat the oil.
- Add the onion, garlic, carrot, potatoes, celery, paprika, and cu minutes
- Saute for 5 minutes.
- Add the lentils and water, stir well. Close and lock the lid.
- Press the CANCEL button to stop the SAUTE function, then select the MANUAL setting and set the cooking time for 3 minutes at HIGH pressure.
- When the timer beeps, use a
- Natural Release
- for 10 minutes.
- Uncover the pot.
- Add the chard and sprinkle with salt and pepper.
- Stir well.
- Let the soup sit for 5 minutes and serve.

MEXICAN TACO SOUP

Serving: 2
Preparation time: 5 minutes
Cooking time: 4 hours
Ingredients:

- 1 lb ground meat, browned
- 8 oz cream cheese
- 10 oz diced tomatoes and chilis
- 1 tbsp of taco seasonings
- 1 cup of chicken broth

Directions:

- Combine all ingredients in the crockpot.
- Cook on low for 4 hours.

Nutrition:

- Calories - 547
- Fat - 43 g
- Carbs - 5 g
- Protein - 33 g

SHREDDED CHICKEN

Preparation + Cooking time: 30 minutes
Serving: 6
Ingredients:

- 3 lbs. boneless, skinless chicken thighs
- 2 cups tomato
- 1 cup chopped yellow onion
- 1 cup chopped red pepper

- 2 tbsp. olive oil
- 2 tbsp. sage
- 2 tbsp. thyme
- salt and pepper to taste

Directions:

- Put your Instant Pot on High and warm the oil in it.
- Add the onion.
- Soften 5 minutes.
- Add the remaining ingredients.
- Seal and cook on Stew for 20 minutes.
- Release the pressure slowly.
- Shred the chicken.

Nutrition:

- Calories - 280
- Fat - 11g
- Carbs - 12g
- Protein - 38g

RICH BUTTERNUT SQUASH SOUP WITH PARSNIPS

Serving: 8
Ingredients:

- 1 large sweet onion, chopped
- 3 large parsnips, peeled and chopped
- 1 large Granny Smith apple, peeled and chopped
- ¼ teaspoon salt
- 1 teaspoon freshly ground black pepper
- 3 cups water
- 2 cups chicken broth, reduced sodium, fat-free
- 3 12-ounce packages frozen butternut squash, thawed
- 2 tablespoons whipping cream
- 1/8 teaspoon paprika
- 1/8 teaspoon ground cu minutes
- ½ cup light sour cream
- Chopped fresh chives (optional

Directions:

- Place the onion, parsnips, apple, salt, pepper, water, broth and squash in the slow cooker. Stir.
- Cover and cook for 6 hours on LOW.
- Puree using an immersion blender until smooth. (A regular blender may also be used. Puree in small batches to prevent spillage. Be careful, liquid is hot! Remove lid insert to allow steam to escape.)
- Stir in the whipping cream, paprika, and cu minutes

- Serve with a dollop of sour cream on top, sprinkled with chives.
- Place the wing tips, chicken pieces, onion, ginger, coriander, cloves, star anise, sugar, fish sauce, and cilantro in the slow cooker.
- Add water until slow cooker is about ¾ full.
- Cover and cook for 8-10 hours on LOW or for 4-6 hours on HIGH.
- Remove chicken (to be added later to noodles) and discard cilantro stems.
- Strain the broth through cheesecloth. Discard the strained solids. All you want is the tasty, clear broth.
- Adjust the taste of the broth with fish sauce and sugar, if needed.

Nutrition:

- Calories - 132
- Fat - 5 g
- Carbs - 30 g
- Protein - 4 g

CREAMY SPINACH SOUP

Preparation + Cooking time: 30 minutes
Serving: 2
Ingredients:

- For soup: 3 cups spinach, chopped
- 1 cup cauliflower, chopped
- 3 cups beef broth
- ½ cup heavy cream
- 2 tbsp butter
- Spices: ¼ tsp sea salt
- ½ tsp black pepper, freshly ground
- 1 tsp garlic powder

Directions:

- Plug in your instant pot and set the stainless steel insert.
- Place spinach in a large sieve and rinse well under running water. Stir well and pour in the broth. Seal the lid and set the steam release handle to the "Sealing" position. Press the "MANUAL" button and set the timer for 10 minutes on high pressure.
- When done, press the €žCancel"button and release the pressure naturally for 10-15
- minutes. Then move the pressure valve to the "Venting" position to release any remaining pressure.
- Carefully, open the lid and stir in two tablespoons of butter.
- Chill for a while.
- Serve immediately.

Nutrition:

- Calories - 286
- Fat - 24.9g
- Carbs - 4.3g
- Protein - 10.3g

LENTIL CHILI

Serving: 4
Ingredients:

- ½ medium onion, diced
- 2 cloves garlic, minced
- ½ jalapeÃ±o, diced, seeds removed
- ½ red pepper, chopped
- ½ yellow pepper, chopped
- ½ large carrot, peeled and diced
- 1 ½ cups vegetable broth
- 1 (15-ounce can tomato sauce
- 1 (15-ounce) can diced tomatoes
- 8 ounces brown lentils, rinsed
- 1 (15-ounce) cans small red kidney beans, rinsed and drained
- 2 tablespoons chili powder
- ½ tablespoon cu minutes
- Salt and black pepper, to taste

Directions:

- Place the onion, garlic, jalapeÃ±o, red pepper, yellow pepper, carrot, vegetable broth, tomato sauce, diced tomatoes, brown lentils, red beans, chili powder, cumin, and salt and black pepper in a slow cooker. Stir well to combine.
- Cover and cook on LOW for 6 hours. Serve warm.

Nutrition:

- Calories - 285
- Fat - 2 g
- Carbs - 50.6 g
- Protein - 19.1 g

FISH AND SEAFOOD

CITRUS-CILANTRO FISH TACOS

Serving: 6-8
Ingredients:

- 6 fish fillets (for example, cod, salmon or tilapia
- 2 medium tomatoes, seeded and diced
- 2 jalapeno peppers, seeded and chopped
- 1 clove garlic, minced
- 1 shallot, minced
- ¼ cup fresh chopped cilantro
- 2 tablespoons lime or lemon juice
- salt, (to taste)
- Shredded cabbage for serving

For paleo taco shells

- 3 tablespoons coconut flour
- 3 tablespoons milled flax seed
- 1 .cup coconut milk

Directions:

- For filling
- Place the fish fillets in the slow cooker.
- Add the other remaining ingredients for the filling, sprinkling and spreading evenly over the fish.
- Cook for 3 to 4 hours on LOW or until fish is easy to flake with a fork.
- Flake and mix thoroughly.
- For the taco shells
- Preheat the oven to 400 F.
- Mix the ingredients together.
- Form a ball and roll out thinly between the parchment paper.
- Cut out circles using the mouth of a jar (about 4 inches diameter).
- Drape the circles over the oven grill to form taco shapes.
- Bake until crispy, about 10 to15 minutes.
- Fill with the fish mixture and serve.
- VARIATION: Use lettuce leaves instead of taco shells.

Nutrition:

- Calories - 166
- Fat - 5.9 g
- Carbs - 10.8 g
- Protein - 18.3 g

SALMON RISOTTO

Serving: 3
Ingredients:

- 1 1/2 Tbsp unsalted butter
- 4 oz Arborio rice
- 2 Tbsp minced onion
- 1 1/2 cups low sodium vegetable broth
- 1/4 cup dry white wine
- 1/8 tsp ground black pepper
- 1/2 lb salmon fillet, cubed

Directions:

- Place a skillet over medium high flame and melt the butter. Add the minced onion and
- saute until Pour the Arborio rice into the slow cooker, followed by the broth, wine, and black pepper.
- Cover and cook for 3 hours on low, stirring once halfway into the cooking time.

- Add the salmon and stir to distribute. Cover and cook for 30 minutes on high or until salmon is cooked through and rice is puffed and tender. Serve warm.

Nutrition:

- Calories - 294

SHRIMP MIX

Preparation time: 10 minutes
Cooking time: 2 hours and 30 minutes
Serving: 4
Ingredients:

- 1 cup chicken stock
- 2 tablespoons olive oil
- 2 teaspoons parsley, chopped
- 2 teaspoons garlic, minced
- 20 shrimp, peeled and deveined

Directions:

- In your slow cooker, mix stock with oil, parsley, garlic and shrimp, toss, cover and cook on Low for 2 hours and 30 minutes.
- Divide into bowls and serve.
- Enjoy!

Nutrition:

- Calories - 162
- Fat - 2
- Carbs - 9
- Protein - 2

CLASSIC SEAFOOD STEW

Serving: 8
Ingredients:

- 10 cups mixed frozen vegetables
- 2 ½ cups marinara sauce
- 3 packets of frozen mixed seafood (12 ounces each
- ½ cup basil leaves
- Salt and pepper
- ¼ cup extra virgin olive oil

Directions:

- Place the onions, mixed vegetables and marinara sauce in the slow cooker and cook for 2-2 ½ hours, until the vegetables are soft.
- Stir in mixed seafood and extra virgin olive oil.

- Cover and cook for 15-20 minutes more, until the seafood is firm.
- Season with salt and pepper and add fresh basil leaves.
- Serve hot over pasta or polenta.

Nutrition:

- Calories - 219
- Fat - 6 g
- Carbs - 19 g
- Protein - 22 g

COD CURRY

Preparation time: 10 minutes
Cooking time: 2 hours
Serving: 6
Ingredients:

- 6 cod fillets, skinless, boneless and cut into medium cubes
- 1 tomato, chopped
- 14 ounces coconut milk
- 2 yellow onions, sliced
- 2 green bell peppers, chopped
- 2 garlic cloves, minced
- ½ teaspoon turmeric powder
- 6 curry leaves
- A pinch of salt and black pepper
- 2 teaspoons cumin, ground
- 2 tablespoons lemon juice
- 1 tablespoons coriander, ground
- 1 tablespoon ginger, grated
- 1 teaspoon hot pepper flakes

Directions:

- In your slow cooker, mix fish cubes with tomato, coconut milk, onions, green bell peppers, garlic, curry leaves, turmeric, salt, pepper, cumin, lemon juice, coriander, ginger and pepper flakes, toss a bit, cover and cook on High for 2 hours.
- Divide into bowls and serve.
- Enjoy!

Nutrition:

- Calories - 201
- Fat - 7
- Carbs - 12
- Protein - 13

FISH AND TOMATOES

Serving: 2

Preparation time: 7 minutes
Cooking time: 3 hours
Ingredients:

- 1/2 bell pepper, sliced
- 1/8 cup low-sodium broth
- 8 oz diced tomatoes
- 1/2 tbsp rosemary
- 1/2 lb cod

Directions:

- Put all the ingredients except the fish in the crock-pot. Add garlic, salt and pepper to taste.
- Season fish with your favorite seasoning and place other ingredient in the pot.
- Cook for 3 hours on low.

Nutrition:

- al Value:
- Calories - 204
- Fat - 16.8g
- Carbs - 5g
- Protein - 25.3g
- Cholesterol - 75mg
- Sodium - 296mg
- Serving suggestions: Season with red pepper flakes for extra spice.

KETO GREEN PESTO TUNA STEAK

Preparation + Cooking time: 40 minutes
Serving: 4
Ingredients:

- 2 tuna steaks; about 1-inch thick
- 3 tablespoon mozzarella; shredded
- 1 cup basil leaves; finely chopped.
- 1 cup cauliflower; finely chopped
- 1/4 cup olive oil
- 2 garlic cloves
- 3 tablespoon butter
- 1 teaspoon sea salt

Directions:

- Plug in the instant pot and set the steam basket. Pour in one cup of water and add tuna steaks in the basket
- Season with salt and seal the lid. Set the steam release handle to the "SEALING" position and press the "MANUAL" button. Cook for 7 minutes on high pressure
- When done, perform a quick release and open the lid. Using oven mitts, gently remove the steam basket and set aside

- Remove the water from the pot and add butter. Press the "SAUTE" button and heat up
- Briefly cook each tuna steak for 3-4 minutes on each side
- Remove from the pot and set aside
- Now; prepare the pesto. Combine the remaining ingredients in a food processor and process until completely smooth. Coat each tuna steak with pesto and place on a small baking sheet lined with some parchment paper
- Bake for 15 minutes at 400 degrees or until lightly brown and crispy. Serve and enjoy.

Nutrition:

- Calories - 484
- Fat - 32.9g
- Carbs - 2g
- Protein - 44.3g

CHEESY TUNA AND NOODLES

Preparation + Cooking time: 10 minutes
Serving: 4
Ingredients:

- ½ cup shredded Cheddar Cheese
- 2 Tuna cans, drained
- 1 cup Water
- ½ cup Heavy Cream
- 4 Zucchini Noodles
- 4 tbsp. Cheddar Cheese

Directions:

- Pour the water into your Instant Pot.
- Place the zoodles, heavy cream, tuna, and cheddar, in a baking dish.
- Stir to combine.
- Place the dish inside the IP.
- Close the lid and cook on HIGH for 3 minutes.
- Divide between 4 bowls.
- Top with parmesan cheese.
- Serve and enjoy!

Nutrition:

- Calories - 210
- Fat - 9.3g
- Carbs - 2g
- Protein - 15g

COD AND ORANGE SAUCE

Preparation + Cooking time: 15 minutes
Serving: 4
Ingredients:

- 4 cod fillets, boneless
- A small ginger piece, grated
- 1 cup white wine
- Juice from 1 orange
- Salt and ground black pepper to taste.
- 4 spring onions, chopped

Directions:

- Add the ginger, wine, and orange juice to the Instant Pot, mix well,
- Place a steamer basket on top.
- Place the cod fillets in the basket. Season with salt and pepper.
- Close and lock the lid. Select MANUAL and cook at HIGH pressure for 7 minutes.
- When the timer goes off, use a Quick Release
- Carefully open the lid.
- Serve the fish with sauce and sprinkle with green onions.

FISH CURRY

Serving: 6
Ingredients:

- 1 1/2 cups chopped onion
- 1 1/2 Tbsp chopped green chilies
- 1 1/2 tsp garlic
- 3 Tbsp shredded coconut
- 1 cup water, divided
- 3 Tbsp olive oil
- 1 1/2 Tbsp mild curry powder
- 1 cup non fat evaporated milk
- 1 1/2 lb catfish or other firm white fish
- 3 Tbsp lime juice
- 4 1/2 Tbsp dried cilantro

Directions:

- Toss together the onion, garlic, coconut, and 4 tablespoons of water in the food processor. Mix until pasty.
- Place a skillet over medium flame and heat the olive oil. Add the curry powder into the skillet and stir fry until fragrant.
- Stir in the onion and saute until Add the milk into the slow cooker, cover, and cook for 1 hour on high.
- Slice the fish into chunks, then place into a bowl and add the cilantro and lime juice. Set aside to marinate for about 20 minutes.
- Add the fish together with the marinade into the slow cooker.
- Cover and cook for 1 hour on high, or until the fish is cooked through.

Nutrition:

- Calories - 282

THYME SHRIMP TACOS

Preparation time: 10 minutes
Cooking time: 2 hours
Serving: 2
Ingredients:

- 2 keto tortillas
- ½ teaspoon Taco seasoning
- 2 tablespoons fresh cilantro, chopped
- 2 oz Cheddar cheese, shredded
- 1 tablespoon salsa
- 7 oz shrimps, peeled
- ½ cup heavy cream
- ½ teaspoon ground coriander
- 1 teaspoon salt
- 1 jalapeno pepper, sliced

Directions:

- Put shrimps, salt, ground coriander, and Taco seasoning in the crockpot.
- Add heavy cream and close the lid.
- Cook shrimps on High for 2 hours.
- After this, fill keto tortillas with shrimps and top with salsa, sliced jalapeno pepper, cilantro, and shredded Cheddar cheese. Fold the tacos.

Nutrition:

- Calories - 420
- Fat - 26.2
- Carbs - 8.7
- Protein - 36.5

CAJUN SHRIMP AND RICE

Serving: 3
Ingredients:

- 14 oz canned diced tomatoes
- ½ cup chopped green bell pepper
- ½ cup chopped onions
- 2 cloves garlic, chopped
- 3 oz long grain and wild rice mix (like Uncle Ben's
- 2 Tbsp water
- 7 oz chicken broth
- ¼ tsp Cajun seasoning or to taste
- ½ lb shrimp, peeled, deveined
- Hot pepper sauce to taste
- Salt to taste

Directions:

- Add tomatoes with juice, onion, broth, bell pepper, rice mixture along with seasoning packet, broth, water, Cajun seasoning and garlic into the slow cooker and stir until well combined.
- Cover and cook for 5-6 hours on Low or for 3 -3 ½ hours on High.
- Add shrimp and stir. Cover and cook for 15 minutes on High.
- When done, fluff with a fork. Drizzle hot pepper sauce on top and serve.

SEAFOOD GUMBO

Preparation + Cooking time: 25 minutes
Serving: 4
Ingredients:

- 12 oz sea bass filets cut into 2" chunks
- 1 lb medium to large raw shrimp, deveined
- Salt and ground black pepper to taste
- 1½ tbsp Cajun or creole seasoning
- 1½ tbsp ghee or avocado oil
- 1 yellow onion, diced
- 2 celery ribs, diced
- ¾ cups bone broth
- 14 oz diced tomatoes
- 1/8 cup tomato paste
- 2 bay leaves
- 1 bell pepper, diced

Directions:

- Rub all sides of the fillets with salt, pepper and half of Cajun or creole seasoning.
- Preheat the Instant Pot by selecting SAUTe. Add and heat the oil or melt ghee
- Add the fish to the pot and cook for 2 minutes per side.
- Remove the fillets from the pot. Add the remaining Cajun or creole seasoning, onions, and celery.
- Saute for 2 minutes until fragrant.
- Add the broth, tomatoes, tomato paste, bay leaves, bell pepper, shrimp and cooked fish.
- Press the CANCEL button to reset the cooking program, then press the MANUAL button and set the cooking time for 5 minutes at HIGH pressure.
- Once pressure cooking is complete, use a Quick Release
- Unlock and carefully open the lid.
- Serve.

CLAMS IN ALMOND MILK SAUCE

Preparation time: 10 minutes
Cooking time: 3 hours
Serving: 5
Ingredients:

- 1 cup almond milk
- ¼ cup tomato juice
- 1 teaspoon lemon zest

- ¼ teaspoon ground nutmeg
- ¼ teaspoon turmeric
- ½ cup clam juice
- 1-pound clams
- 1 teaspoon kosher salt
- 1 teaspoon ground black pepper
- 1 teaspoon cornstarch
- 2 oz minced garlic

Directions:

- Combine the almond milk with the cornstarch and stir it until smooth.
- Then pour the mixture into the slow cooker. Add the tomato juice, lemon zest, ground nutmeg, turmeric, calm juice, kosher salt, ground black pepper, and minced garlic.
- Mix and close the lid. Cook the sauce on HIGH for 1 hour.
- Stir it every 20 minutes.
- When the sauce gets little bit thick, it is cooked. Add the clams and stir.
- Close the lid and cook it on LOW for 2 more hours. Then Enjoy!

Nutrition:

- Calories - 105
- Fat - 1
- Carbs - 23
- Protein - 2

STEAMED MUSSELS WITH THYME

Preparation + Cooking time: 20 minutes
Serving: 4
Ingredients:

- 1 lb mussels, cleaned
- 2 cups fish stock
- 5 garlic cloves, crushed
- 2 tbsp lemon juice, freshly squeezed
- 3 tbsp butter
- ¼ cup Parmesan cheese, grated
- Spices: 1 tsp dried thyme
- ½ tsp chili flakes
- 2 tbsp fresh parsley, finely chopped

Directions:

- Rinse well the mussels under running water and remove any dirt.
- Drain and set aside.
- Plug in the instant pot and press the "Saute" button. Grease the inner pot with butter and add garlic. Saute for 2-3 minutes and then pour in the stock. Drizzle with lemon juice and season with thyme, chili flakes, and parsley.
- Place mussels in a steam basket and Press the "MANUAL" button and set the timer for 5 minutes on high pressure.

- When done, perform a quick release and open the lid. Remove any mussels that didn't open and serve immediately.
- Calories - 207
- Fat - 17.1g
- Carbs - 5.6g
- Protein - 17.1g

COD FILLETS

Preparation time: 11 minutes
Cooking time: 3 hours
Serving: 5
Ingredients:

- 2 medium tomatoes, sliced
- 1 teaspoon minced garlic
- 1 teaspoon onion powder
- 1 tablespoon ground coriander
- 1 teaspoon cilantro
- 1 teaspoon olive oil
- ½ tablespoon kosher salt
- 2-pounds cod fillet
- 2 tablespoons mayo

Directions:

- Combine the minced garlic, onion powder, ground coriander, cilantro, and kosher salt together.
- Stir the spices and add the mayo.
- Cut the cod fillets into the serving pieces. Rub every cod fillet with the mayo mixture from the each side with the help of your hands.
- Then make the layer from the sliced tomatoes in the slow cooker bowl. Put the cod fillets there and close the lid. Cook the cod fillet for 3 hours on HIGH.
- When the dish is cooked, Enjoy!

Nutrition:

- Calories - 147
- Fat - 1.8
- Carbs - 2.97
- Protein - 28

STUFFED TROUT

Preparation time: 20 minutes
Cooking time: 4 hours
Serving: 5
Ingredients:

- 16 oz whole trout, peeled
- ½ cup sweet corn

- ¼ cup rice, cooked
- 1 sweet pepper, chopped
- 1 tablespoon salt
- 1 teaspoon thyme
- 1 teaspoon ground black pepper
- ½ teaspoon paprika
- 1 tablespoon olive oil
- 1 tablespoon sour cream
- ¼ cup cream cheese
- 3 lemon wedges
- 2 tablespoons chives

Directions:

- Combine the sweet corn and cooked rice together. Add the chopped sweet pepper.
- Then sprinkle with the chives and salt. Stir the mixture well. Combine the thyme, ground black pepper, paprika, sour cream, olive oil, and cream cheese together.
- Put the trout on the foil and rub it with the cream cheese mixture carefully. Then fill the fish with the rice mixture. Put the lemon wedges over the trout and wrap it in the foil.
- Close the slow cooker lid and cook the fish for 4 hours on HIGH.
- When the fish is cooked, remove it from the slow cooker and

Nutrition:

- Calories - 255
- Fat - 13.9
- Carbs - 13.57
- Protein - 22

CHICKEN AND POULTRY

SHREDDED CHICKEN WITH SHIITAKE RECIPE

Preparation + Cooking time: 30 minutes
Serving: 5
Ingredients:

- 6 shiitake mushrooms
- 1-pound chicken breast; boneless and skinless
- 1/2 teaspoon stevia powder
- 1 ½ cup chicken stock
- 1 spring onion; finely chopped
- 1 tablespoon light soy sauce
- 4 tablespoon sesame oil
- 2 teaspoon rice vinegar
- 2 tablespoon butter
- 2 tablespoon dark soy sauce
- 1/2 teaspoon pepper; freshly ground.
- 1/2 teaspoon chili flakes
- 1 tablespoon fresh ginger; grated

Directions:

- In a small bowl, whisk together oil, dark soy sauce, light soy sauce, stevia powder, rice vinegar, ginger, chili flakes, and pepper. Optionally, add some salt and set aside
- Rinse the meat and place on a cutting board. Chop into smaller pieces and place at
- the bottom of your instant pot. Add spring onions and pour in the stock.
- Seal the lid and set the steam release handle to the "SEALING" position. Press the "POULTRY" button and cook for 10 minutes
- When you hear the cooker's end signal, perform a quick pressure release and open the lid. Remove the chicken from the pot and place in a deep bowl. Drizzle with the prepared soy mixture and shred with two forks, Set aside.
- Remove the remaining stock from the pot and press the "SAUTE" button. Grease the inner pot with butter and heat up
- Add shiitake and briefly cook - for 3-4 minutes, stirring constantly.
- Now add the meat and give it a good stir. Cook for another 5 minutes. When done; remove from the pot and serve immediately

Nutrition:

- Calories - 299
- Fat - 18.1g
- Carbs - 11.3g
- Protein - 21.7g

MOROCCAN RISOTTO

Preparation + Cooking time: 35 minutes
Serving: 2
Ingredients:

- 1-pound chicken breast; boneless and skinless, cut into bite-sized pieces
- 2 cups cauliflower; chopped into florets
- 1 teaspoon fresh oregano
- 1 pinch saffron
- 2 cups chicken stock
- 3 tablespoon olive oil
- 1 spring onion; finely chopped
- 1/2 teaspoon white pepper
- 1 teaspoon turmeric powder
- 2 teaspoon salt

Directions:

- Rinse well the meat and pat dry with a kitchen paper, Set aside.
- Plug in the instant pot and press the "SAUTE" button. Heat the inner pot and add olive oil and onions. Briefly cook, for 3-4 minutes
- Now add the remaining ingredients and stir well. Securely lock the lid and adjust the
- steam release handle. Press the "MANUAL" button. Set the timer for 15 minutes
- When you hear the end signal, release the pressure naturally and open the lid a large platter and chop the cauliflower into small piece. Sprinkle with some more saffron and serve immediately.

Nutrition:

- Calories - 476
- Fat - 27.3g
- Carbs - 3.9g
- Protein - 50.9g

WHITE CHICKEN WITH CAULIFLOWER

Preparation + Cooking time: 30 minutes
Serving: 4
Ingredients:

- 1 Butter Stick
- 4 Chicken Breasts, cubed
- 2 cups Cauliflower Florets
- 2 cups Heavy Cream
- 8 ounces Cream Cheese
- 1 tsp minced Garlic
- 1 tbsp. chopped Basil

Directions:

- Preheat your Instant Pot on SAUTE.
- Melt the butter inside.
- Whisk together the cream cheese and heavy cream inside.
- Stir in the remaining ingredients and close the lid.
- Cook on HIGH for 15 minutes.
- Do a quick pressure release.
- Serve and enjoy!

Nutrition:

- Calories - 700
- Fat - 40g
- Carbs - 5g
- Protein - 70g

BRUNSWICK STEW

Serving: 8
Ingredients:

- 2 potatoes, peeled and cubed
- 8 oz frozen okra
- 8 oz frozen Lima beans
- 8 oz frozen corn
- 2 1/2 cups diced cooked chicken breast
- 3/4 Tbsp coconut sugar or noncaloric sweetener
- 1/3 tsp rosemary
- 1/6 tsp cloves

- 1/6 tsp freshly ground black pepper
- 1 bay leaf
- 3 cups low sodium chicken broth
- 12 oz unsalted sliced peeled tomatoes, not drained

Directions:

- Combine the potatoes and frozen okra, Lima beans, and corn into the slow cooker.
- Gently toss in the chicken, cloves, rosemary, pepper, sugar, and bay leaf. Add the chicken broth and tomatoes together with its juices.
- Cover and cook for 8 hours on low. Take out the bay leaf before serving.

Nutrition:

- Calories - 203

GOOSE AND CHILI SAUCE

Preparation + Cooking time: 25 minutes
Serving: 2
Ingredients:

- 1 lb goose breast, skinless, boneless and cut into 1/6 inch slices
- ¼ cup extra virgin olive oil
- 2 tsp garlic, chopped
- 1 sweet onion, chopped
- Salt and black pepper to taste
- ¼ cup sweet chili sauce
- ½ cup water

Directions:

- Select the SAUTe setting on the Instant Pot and heat the oil.
- Add the garlic and onion, saute for about 2 minutes.
- Add the goose breast slices, pepper and salt, stir and cook for 2 minutes on both sides.
- Pour the chili sauce and water, stir.
- Press the CANCEL button to reset the cooking program, then select the MANUAL setting and set the cooking time for 5 minutes at HIGH pressure.
- Once cooking is complete, use a Quick Release
- Unlock and carefully open the lid.
- Serve.

SPANISH CHICKEN

Preparation time: 10 minutes
Cooking time: 7.5 hours
Serving: 2
Ingredients:

- ¼ cup Spanish olives, sliced
- 1 tablespoon tomato sauce

- ½ teaspoon dried oregano
- ¾ teaspoon chili flakes
- 1 tablespoon olive oil
- ½ teaspoon grated onion
- ¾ cup organic almond milk
- 7 oz chicken breast, skinless, boneless, chopped

Directions:

- Mix up together almond milk, grated onion, olive oil, chili flakes, dried oregano, and tomato sauce.
- When the mixture is homogenous, pour it in the crockpot.
- Add Spanish olives and chicken breast.
- Close the lid and cook chicken for 7.5 hours on Low.

Nutrition:

- Calories - 242
- Fat - 14.3
- Carbs - 1.8
- Protein - 26.2.

CURRIED CHICKEN WITH TOMATOES, SPINACH AND YOGURT

Preparation + Cooking time: 60 minutes
Serving: 8
Ingredients:

- 1 ½ cups Yogurt
- 4 pounds Chicken, cubed
- 2 Tomatoes, chopped
- 4 ounces Spinach
- 1/3 pound Curry Paste
- 1 tbsp. Olive Oil
- 1 Onion, sliced
- 1 tbsp. chopped Coriander

Directions:

- Combine the chicken, curry paste, and yogurt, in a bowl.
- Cover, and let marinate in the fridge for 30 minutes.
- Heat the oil in the IP on SAUTE.
- Cook the onions until soft.
- Add tomatoes and cook for another minute.
- Pour the chicken mixture over.
- Stir in spinach and coriander.
- Lock the lid and cook on HIGH for 15 minutes.
- Do a quick pressure release.
- Serve and enjoy!

Nutrition:

- Calories - 423
- Fat - 18g
- Carbs - 6.8g
- Protein - 40g

CHICKEN BREAST WITH OLIVES

Preparation time: 10 minutes
Cooking time: 7 hours
Serving: 4
Ingredients:

- 3 kalamata olives
- 1-pound chicken breast
- 3 garlic cloves, roughly chopped
- 1 tablespoon basil, chopped
- ½ teaspoon salt
- 1 teaspoon smoked paprika
- 1/3 cup coconut oil
- ½ teaspoon dried marjoram

Directions:

- In the shallow bowl, mix up together dried marjoram, smoked paprika, salt, and basil. Chop the kalamata olive roughly.
- Make the small cuts in the chicken breast and fill them with olives and chopped garlic.
- The carefully rub the chicken breast with the spice mixture and Add coconut oil and close the lid.
- Cook the chicken for 7 hours on Low.
- When the chicken is cooked, slice it into the.

Nutrition:

- Calories - 295
- Fat - 21.5
- Carbs - 1.3
- Protein - 24.3

THAI BOWL

Preparation time: 15 minutes
Cooking time: 4 hours 15 minutes
Serving: 7
Ingredients:

- 9 oz turkey fillet
- 5 oz coconut milk
- 1 teaspoon salt
- 1 teaspoon turmeric

- 2 tablespoons peanut butter
- 6 oz noodles, cooked
- 6 oz red cabbage, sliced
- 1 jalapeno pepper
- 1 tablespoon oregano
- 1 tablespoon tomato paste
- 1 teaspoon fresh parsley, chopped

Directions:

- Chop the turkey fillet roughly and put it in the slow cooker bowl. Combine the coconut milk with salt, turmeric, peanut butter, oregano, tomato paste, and fresh parsley.
- Mix well. After this, sprinkle the turkey fillet with the coconut milk mixture. Slice the jalapeno pepper and add the sliced jalapeno into the slow cooker and close the lid.
- Cook the turkey for 4 hours on HIGH. Then add the cooked noodles and stir carefully with a spatula.
- Cook the dish on HIGH for 15 minutes more.
- Then Enjoy!

Nutrition:

- Calories - 279
- Fat - 22
- Carbs - 11.6
- Protein - 9

CHICKEN AND SALSA FOR TORTILLAS

Serving: 6
Ingredients:

- 1 packet of taco mix seasoning
- 4 chicken breasts
- Cooking spray
- 1 cup salsa of your choice
- 1 can cream of chicken soup
- ½ cup sour cream

Directions:

- Rub the seasoning on the chicken.
- Spray the slow cooker with cooking spray and put the chicken in it.
- Combine the rest of the ingredients in a bowl and spread over the chicken.
- Cover and cook for 3-4 hours on HIGH
- Shred the chicken and stir it back into the sauce.
- Serve as desired.

ROOT BEER CHICKEN WINGS

Serving: 8
Preparation time: 5 minutes

Cooking time: 15 minutes
Ingredients:

- 2 pounds chicken wings
- 2 cans of root beer
- ¼ cup sugar
- ¼ cup soy sauce

Directions:

- Place all ingredients in the Instant Pot.
- Give a good stir.
- Close the lid and press the Poultry button.
- Adjust the cooking time to 10 minutes.
- Do quick pressure release.

Nutrition:

- Calories - 229
- Carbs - 18.2g
- Protein - 25.5 g
- Fat - 5.5g

CHICKEN ADOBO

Preparation + Cooking time: 40 minutes
Serving: 2-4
Ingredients:

- 4 chicken drumsticks
- ½ tsp kosher salt
- 1 tsp ground black pepper
- 2 tbsp olive oil
- ¼ cup white vinegar
- 1/3 cup soy sauce
- ¼ cup sugar
- 1 onion, chopped
- 5 cloves garlic, crushed
- 2 bay leaves

Directions:

- Select SAUTe on high heat. Wait 1 minute and add the oil to the bottom of the pot.
- Season the legs with salt and ½ teaspoon pepper.
- Add the chicken drumsticks to the Instant Pot and brown for 4 minutes on each side.
- Add the vinegar, soy sauce, sugar, onion, garlic, bay leaves and ½ teaspoon pepper.
- Close and lock the lid. Select MANUAL and cook at HIGH pressure for 10 minutes.
- When the timer goes off, use a
- Quick Release
- . Carefully open the lid.
- Select the SAUTe setting on high heat and simmer for 10 minutes to reduce the sauce.

- Press the CANCEL button to stop the cooking program.
- Remove the bay leaves. Serve.

BARBECUE CHEDDAR CHICKEN

Serving: 2
Ingredients:

- 2 chicken breasts
- 1 cup spicy barbecue sauce
- Salt and pepper to taste
- 2 ounce sharp cheddar cheese, shredded
- Spray slow cooker with cooking spray.
- Season chicken breasts with salt and pepper. Place chicken breasts in the slow cooker.
- Pour BBQ sauce on top.
- Cook on HIGH for 4 hours or 7-8 hours on LOW.
- Shred chicken.
- Place chicken back in slow cooker. Top with the shredded cheese. Slow cook for about 10 more minutes until the cheese is melted.
- Place cheesy chicken in bun. Top with bacon strips and serve.

Directions:

- Place the chicken in the slow cooker.
- Top with the barbecue sauce and season to taste with salt and pepper. Stir the ingredients gently to combine, using a wooden spatula.
- Cover, and cook on HIGH for 3 hours.
- After 2 hours and 45 minutes, open the lid and top with the cheese.
- Close the lid; cook on "HIGH" for 15 minutes, until the cheese is melted.
- Serve, and enjoy!

Nutrition:

- Calories - 291
- Fat - 17 g
- Carbs - 5.2 g
- Protein - 29 g

MUGHLAI ALMOND CHICKEN

Preparation + Cooking time: 25 minutes
Serving: 6
Ingredients:

- 2 lbs chicken breasts, skinless and boneless
- 1 medium-sized onion, chopped
- ½ cup toasted almonds
- 1 cup heavy cream
- 3 garlic cloves, peeled
- 1 tbsp olive oil
- Spices: 1 tsp garam masala powder

- 1 tbsp fresh ginger, grated
- 1 tsp red pepper flakes
- 1 tsp coriander powder
- 2 cardamom pods
- 1 bay leaf
- 1 small cinnamon stick

Directions:

- Combine garlic, almonds, and giinger in a food processor. Add 2 tablespoons of water and pulse until combined and creamy.
- Set aside,
- Plug in your instant pot and grease the stainless steel insert with olive oil. Add chicken breasts and cook for 3-4 minutes on each side, or until lightly browned.
- Now, add all the remaining spice and cook for 2-3 minutes more, stirring constantly.
- Add onions and heavy cream. Give it a good stir and securely lock the lid.
- Adjust the steam release handle and press the "MANUAL" button. Set the timer for 8 minues and cook on "High" pressure.
- When you hear the cooker's end signal.
- Release the pressure naturally.
- Open the pot and Enjoy!

Nutrition:

- Calories - 439
- Fat - 25.1g
- Carbs - 4.1g
- Protein - 48.4g

MARINARA AND CHEESE STEWED CHICKEN

Preparation + Cooking time: 25 minutes
Serving: 6
Ingredients:

- 1 ½ pounds Chicken Meat (boneless thighs or breasts), cubed
- 15 ounces Chicken Broth
- 8 ounces Cheese (Monterey Jack or Cheddar), shredded
- 15 ounces Keto Marinara Sauce
- Salt and Pepper, to taste

Directions:

- Mix everything in your Instant Pot.
- Cover and lock the lid.
- Choose the MANUAL cooking mode and cook on HIGH for 15 minutes.
- Do a quick pressure release.
- Serve and enjoy!

Nutrition:

- Calories - 270
- Fat - 17g
- Carbs - 2g
- Protein - 21.5g

GARLIC AND SAGE MILK CHICKEN

Serving: 4-6
Ingredients:

- 1 whole chicken (about 4-5 pounds, cleaned
- Salt and pepper
- ¼ cup lightly packed fresh sage leaves
- 1 cup apple cider or apple juice
- 10 cloves garlic, peeled and smashed
- 1 ¾ cups whole milk

Directions:

- Pat the chicken dry with a paper towel. Season with salt, pepper. Place sage leaves into the cavity.
- Pour the cider over the chicken.
- Place garlic cloves over the chicken and pour the milk over it.
- Cover and cook for 4 to 6 hours on LOW until internal temperature is above 165°F on an instant read meat thermometer.
- Remove garlic cloves before carving.

Nutrition:

- Calories - 315
- Fat - 35.2 g
- Carbs - 21.3 g
- Protein - 25 g

SWEET CHICKEN LEG STEW

Preparation + Cooking time: 35 minutes
Serving: 4
Ingredients:

- 4 medium-sized chicken legs
- 1 cup diced canned tomatoes; sugar-free
- 2 garlic cloves; whole
- 1 red bell pepper; chopped
- 2 cups mushrooms; sliced
- 3 tablespoon fresh parsley
- 2 tablespoon balsamic vinegar
- 3 tablespoon avocado oil
- 1 onion; finely chopped
- 3 celery stalks; chopped.
- 4 cups chicken broth

- 1 teaspoon dried oregano
- 1/4 teaspoon red pepper flakes
- 2 tablespoon fresh basil; finely chopped
- 1 teaspoon black pepper
- 1 teaspoon fresh thyme; finely chopped
- 1 teaspoon salt

Directions:

- Place the meat in a large colander and rinse thoroughly under cold running water. Dry with a kitchen paper and rub each piece with salt and pepper
- Plug in the instant pot and press the "SAUTE" button. Heat the oil and add chicken thighs in a couple of batches. Brown on all sides, for 3-4 minutes. Remove from the pot and set aside.
- In a deep bowl, combine onions, peppers, celery stalks, and mushrooms. Season with some salt and mix well. Now add garlic and season with oregano and red pepper flakes. Toss well to combine and continue to cook for another 2 minutes.
- Finally, add the remaining ingredients and seal the lid
- Set the steam release handle to the "SEALING" position and press the "MANUAL" button. Set the timer for 15 minutes on high pressure
- When done, perform a quick release and open the lid. Serve and enjoy.

Nutrition:

- Calories - 267
- Fat - 6.5g
- Carbs - 7.7g
- Protein - 40.2g

BEEF, PORK AND LAMB

CILANTRO MEAT BOWL

Preparation time: 15 minutes
Cooking time: 13 hours
Serving: 10
Ingredients:

- 1 cup cilantro
- 11 oz pork chops
- 8 oz beef brisket
- 1 tablespoon rosemary
- 1 teaspoon ground black pepper
- 1 teaspoon salt
- 1 teaspoon paprika
- 1 cup red onion
- 6 oz sweet yellow pepper, chopped
- 2 tablespoons lemon juice
- 1 teaspoon olive oil
- 1 teaspoon oregano

- 4 oz celery stalk, chopped
- 6 oz salsa
- ½ chili pepper

Directions:

- Wash the cilantro carefully and chop it. Chop the pork chops into cubes.
- Sprinkle the meat with the rosemary. Combine the chopped pork cubes with the beef brisket. Add ground black pepper, salt, paprika, lemon juice, and salsa and marinate it for 10 minutes.
- Then Add the red onion, chili pepper, chopped celery stalk, and sweet yellow pepper.
- Sprinkle the mixture with the oregano and olive oil. Cover the mixture with the chopped cilantro and close the lid.
- Cook the meat mixture on LOW for 13 hours.
- When the meat is cooked, stir it carefully with a wooden spoon. Serve the meat in bowls.
- Enjoy!

Nutrition:

- Calories - 134
- Fat - 7.4
- Carbs - 4.58
- Protein - 12

MEXICAN STYLE STUFFED PEPPERS

Preparation time: 5 minutes
Cooking time: 15 minutes
Serving: 4
Ingredients:

- 1 cup cook brown rice
- 1 tomato, diced
- 1 can tomato sauce
- 1 egg
- 1 pound ground beef
- 1 small onion, diced
- 1/2 teaspoon dried parsley
- 1/2 teaspoon garlic powder
- 1/2 teaspoon oregano
- 4 bell peppers
- Mozzarella cheese, shredded
- Black pepper and salt to taste

Directions:

- Slice off the top of the peppers.
- In a mixing bowl, mix the egg, beef, rice, tomato, onion, parsley, garlic powder, oregano, pepper, and salt.
- Stuffed beef mixture into the peppers.
- Take your Instant Pot and open the top lid.

- Pour 1 cup water and 2/3 tomato sauce. Arrange a trivet or steamer basket inside.
- Place the peppers over the trivet/basket. Top with the remaining sauce.
- Close the top lid and seal the pressure valve.
- Press "MANUAL" setting with 15 minutes of cooking time and "HIGH" pressure mode.
- Press "NPR" function to release the pressure slowly in a natural way.
- Open the lid;

Nutrition:

- Calories - 516
- Fat - 16g
- Carbs - 46g
- Sodium - 478mg
- Protein - 37g

MEXICAN SALSA CHUCK ROAST

Serving: 6-8
Ingredients:

- Cooking spray
- 3 pounds chuck roast
- 4 cups chunky salsa (medium
- Tortillas
- Mexican cheese
- Toppings of your choice, such as diced tomato, avocado, sweet onion

Directions:

- Spray the slow cooker and set it to HIGH.
- Put the chuck roast in the cooker and cover with the salsa.
- Cover and cook on HIGH for 2 hours.
- Turn the setting to LOW, and cook for 4-5 more hours.
- Take out the roast from the cooker and shred it in a bowl.
- Add the remaining juice from the cooker to the roast as per you liking.
- Warm the tortillas in the microwave until soft, and spoon about 2 tablespoons of the meat mixture in the center.
- Add cheese and the toppings of your choice.
- Roll and eat!

Nutrition:

- Calories - 324
- Fat - 8.5 g
- Carbs - 10.1 g
- Protein - 50.2 g

PORK CHOPS AND BUTTERED VEGETABLES

Serving: 4
Ingredients:

- 4-6 pork chops
- ¼ cup onion, chopped
- ¼ cup garlic, minced
- 1 bunch of parsley, chopped
- ¼ cup of green bell pepper, diced
- ¼ cup of red bell pepper, diced
- 1 cup tomatoes, diced
- 1 tablespoon black peppercorns, whole
- ¼ cup butter
- 1 cup green peas
- 1 cup carrots, diced
- 1 cup butternut squash, diced
- 1 cup corn kernels

Directions:

- Arrange the pork chops in the slow cooker, and add the onion, garlic, parsley, green bell pepper, red bell pepper, tomatoes and whole peppercorns.
- Cook for 7 hours on low.
- Melt the butter in a medium skillet, and lightly fry the green peas, carrots, butternut squash, and corn.
- Serve pork chops together with buttered vegetables and rice.

Nutrition:

- Calories - 483
- Fat - 18.4 g
- Carbs - 35.8 g
- Protein - 44.2 g

STUFFED LAMB WITH ONIONS

Preparation time: 15 minutes
Cooking time: 6 hours
Serving: 9
Ingredients:

- 3-pounds lamb fillet
- 5 medium onions
- 3 garlic cloves
- 1 carrot
- 1 tablespoon ground black pepper
- 1 tablespoon olive oil
- ¼ cup sour cream
- 1 tablespoon salt
- 1 teaspoon rosemary

Directions:

- Peel the onions and slice them. Then peel the garlic cloves and mince them.
- Combine the sliced onions with the minced garlic.

- Make a "pocket" in the lamb fillet and fill it with the onion mixture. Peel the carrot and chop it then stuff it into the lamb as well.
- After this, secure the lamb fillet with toothpicks. Rub the lamb fillet with the ground
- black pepper, olive oil, sour cream salt, and rosemary.
- Wrap the prepared meat in the foil and put in the slow cooker. Cook the meat on HIGH for 6 hours. Then remove the meat from the slow cooker and discard the foil.
- Serve it!

Nutrition:

- Calories - 440
- Fat - 27.7
- Carbs - 8
- Protein - 38

CREAMY SOUR PORK CHOPS

Preparation + Cooking time: 45 minutes
Serving: 6
Ingredients:

- 4 pork chops, boneless
- 1 cup cream cheese
- ¼ cup heavy cream
- 1 cup sour cream
- 3 tbsp gorgonzola cheese
- 2 tbsp Parmesan cheese
- ½ cup milk
- 1 cup button mushrooms
- 2 tbsp butter
- ¼ cup vegetable stock
- 1 celery stalk, chopped
- 3 tbsp fresh parsley, finely chopped
- Spices: ½ tsp white pepper
- 1 tsp dried rosemary
- ¼ tsp dried oregano

Directions:

- Place the meat in the pot and pour in enough water to cover. Seal the lid and set the steam release handle to the "Sealing" position. Press the "Meat" button and cook for 9 minutes on high pressure.
- When done, perform a quick pressure release and open the lid. Remove the meat and the water from the pot and press the "Saute" button.
- Grease the inner pot with one tablespoon of butter and heat up. Add mushrooms and cook for 5-6 minutes, stirring constantly. Now add cheese, heavy cream, sour cream, and pour in the milk and the stock.
- Sprinkle with pepper, rosemary, and oregano.
- Gently simmer for 5-6 minutes, stirring constantly. Remove from the pot and chill for a while. Now add the remaining butte rin the pot and add chopped celery stalk.
- Cook for 4-5 minutes, stirring constantly.

- Finally, add the meat and brown for 3-4 minutes on each side.
- Serve with the cheese mixture.

Nutrition:

- Calories - 482
- Fat - 34.3g
- Carbs - 4.5g
- Protein - 38.6g

BEEF SHANK

Preparation time: 20 minutes
Cooking time: 9 hours
Serving: 6
Ingredients:

- 5 garlic cloves
- 2 oz fresh rosemary
- 2 yellow onion
- 2 tablespoons ghee
- 1 teaspoon salt
- 17 oz beef shank
- 1 cup beef stock
- 1 teaspoon thyme
- 2 oz tomato paste
- 1 teaspoon ground black pepper
- 1 teaspoon ground coriander
- 1 teaspoon white pepper

Directions:

- Peel the garlic cloves and smash them.
- Chop the rosemary and yellow onion. Put the ghee in the skillet and add the pork shank. Roast the meat on the medium heat for 10 minutes. Stir frequently.
- Sprinkle the beef shank with the garlic cloves.
- Add salt, beef stock, thyme, tomato paste, ground black pepper, ground coriander, and white pepper. Stir the dish gently and close the slow cooker lid.
- Cook the beef shank on LOW for 9 hours. Stir the meat gently occasionally. Remove the prepared beef shank from the slow cooker and cool slighty.
- Serve!

Nutrition:

- Calories - 151
- Fat - 3.8
- Carbs - 9.49
- Protein - 20

PORK SHOULDER

Preparation time: 10 minutes
Cooking time: 7 hours
Serving: 4
Ingredients:

- 2 and ½ pounds pork shoulder
- 4 cups chicken stock
- ½ cup coconut aminos
- ¼ cup white vinegar
- 2 tablespoons chili sauce
- Juice from 1 lime
- 1 tablespoon ginger, grated
- 1 tablespoon Chinese 5 spice
- 2 cup by portabella mushrooms, sliced
- A pinch of salt and black pepper
- 1 zucchini, sliced

Directions:

- In your slow cooker, mix pork shoulder with stock, aminos, vinegar, chili sauce, lime juice, ginger, 5 spice, mushrooms, zucchini, salt and pepper, toss a bit, cover and cook on Low for 7 hours.
- Divide pork between plates and serve.
- Enjoy!

Nutrition:

- Calories - 342
- Fat - 6
- Carbs - 27
- Protein - 18

SWEET GARLIC PORK

Preparation + Cooking time: 45 minutes
Serving: 6
Ingredients:

- 2 lbs pork chops
- ½ cup celery stalks, chopped
- 2 large onions, finely chopped
- 4 garlic cloves
- 1 cup cherry tomatoes
- ¼ cup soy sauce
- 3 tbsp butter
- 3 tbsp apple cider vinegar
- Spices: 1 tsp salt
- 2 tbsp stevia crystal
- ½ tsp ginger powder
- ½ tsp chili flakes

Directions:

- Rinse well the meat and pat dry each piece with some kitchen paper. Place on a large cutting board and remove the bones. Chop into bite-sized pieces and place in a deep bowl. Sprinkle with salt, ginger, and chili flakes. Drizzle with soy sauce and set aside.
- Plug in the instant pot and press the "Saute" button. Grease the inner pot with butter and heat up. Add onions, garlic, and celery stalks. Cook for 3-4 minutes, stirring constantly. Now add cherry tomatoes and sprinkle with stevia. Continue to cook for 5 minutes or until soft.
- Finally, add the meat and drizzle with apple cider vinegar. Stir fry for another 4-5 minutes and then pour in one cup of water.
- Press the "Cancel" button and seal the lid. Set the steam release handle to the "Sealing" position and press the "MANUAL" button.
- Set the timer for 10 minutes on high pressure.when done, release the pressure naturally and open the lid.
- Optionally, sprinkle with freshly chopped parsley and serve immediately.

Nutrition:

- Calories - 569
- Fat - 43.5g
- Carbs - 5.3g
- Protein - 35.6g

PORK ROAST WITH WALNUT BRUSSELS SPROUTS

Serving: 8
Ingredients:

- 4 cups Brussels sprouts, halved
- 4 cloves garlic, crushed and minced
- ½ cup pancetta, cubed
- 2 tablespoons olive oil
- 1 teaspoon salt
- 1 teaspoon black pepper
- 2 teaspoons rubbed sage
- 1 fresh rosemary sprig
- 2 pounds pork tenderloin roast
- 1 cup chicken stock
- ½ cup walnuts, chopped
- ½ cup Brie cheese

Directions:

- Place the Brussels sprouts, garlic, and pancetta in the slow cooker. Drizzle with the olive oil and season with salt, black pepper, rubbed sage, and rosemary. Toss to mix.
- Add the tenderloin roast to the slow cooker, and pour in the chicken stock.
- Cover and cook on low for 8 hours.
- Remove the tenderloin from the slow cooker and allow it to rest before slicing.
- Meanwhile, add the walnuts and Brie cheese. Mix well, cover and cook an additional 10 minutes before serving.

Nutrition:

- Calories - 407.2
- Fat - 24.5 g
- Carbs - 5.1 g
- Protein - 41 g

BEEF TOMATO PASTA

Preparation time: 5 minutes
Cooking time: 16 minutes
Serving: 5
Ingredients:

- 1 pound ground beef
- Cooking oil
- 3 ½ cups tomato and basil sauce
- 2 cups water
- Salt and pepper to taste
- ¼ cup onion, chopped
- ¼ cup garlic, minced
- 8 ounce whole wheat pasta, uncooked
- Parmesan cheese, grated to taste

Directions:

- Take your Instant Pot and open the top lid.
- Press "SAUTE" mode.
- Add the oil and heat it; stir-cook the beef until evenly brown for 3-4 minutes.
- Add the onion and garlic; stir-cook for 4 minutes. Mix the sauce, water and pasta.
- Close the top lid and seal the pressure valve.
- Press "MANUAL" setting with 9 minutes of cooking time and "HIGH" pressure mode.
- Press "QPR" function to release the pressure.
- Open the lid; Enjoy!

Nutrition:

- Calories - 318
- Fat - 11g
- Carbs - 27g
- Sodium - 348mg
- Protein - 26g

INSTANT CHEDDAR BEEF HASH

Preparation + Cooking time: 20 minutes
Serving: 4
Ingredients:

- 1-pound ground beef
- 1 medium-sized green bell pepper; chopped

- 1 cup cauliflower; chopped.
- 1 small celery stalk; chopped
- 1 tablespoon fresh parsley; finely chopped
- 1 tablespoon olive oil
- 1 cup cheddar cheese
- 1/2 teaspoon black pepper; freshly ground.
- 1/2 teaspoon smoked paprika; ground.
- 1 teaspoon sea salt

Directions:

- Plug the instant pot and press the "SAUTE" button. Grease the stainless steel insert with olive oil. Add ground beef and cook for 5 minutes, or until lightly browned
- Now; add bell pepper, cauliflower, and parsley. Add about 1/4 cup of water and continue to cook for another 5 minutes, or until vegetables are tender. Sprinkle all with smoked paprika, salt, and pepper.
- Add the cheese on top and allow it to melt
- Turn off the pot and a
- large slotted spoon. Optionally, top with sour cream and enjoy immediately

Nutrition:

- Calories - 373
- Fat - 2.1g
- Carbs - 3.1g
- Protein - 42.4g

HEARTY PORK RIBS

Preparation time: 12 hours and 10 minutes
Cooking time: 6 hours
Serving: 4
Ingredients:

- 1 whole chicken, cut into medium pieces
- 1 tablespoon olive oil
- 1 and ½ tablespoons lemon zest, grated
- 1 cup chicken stock
- 1 tablespoon thyme, chopped
- 1 teaspoon cinnamon powder
- Salt and black pepper to the taste
- 1 tablespoon cumin, ground
- 2 teaspoons garlic powder
- 2 chicken breasts, skinless and boneless
- 1 tablespoon ghee
- 1 tablespoon olive oil
- ½ cup yellow onion, chopped
- 14 ounces chicken stock
- Salt and black pepper to the taste
- A pinch of red pepper flakes
- 1 tablespoon parsley, chopped

- 3 cups broccoli florets
- 4 ounces coconut cream

Directions:

- Put your ribs in a big bowl, add white vinegar and water, toss, cover and keep in the fridge for 12 hours.
- Drain ribs, season with black pepper to the taste, garlic powder and Chinese 5 spice and rub well.
- Place ribs in your slow cooker and add apple cider vinegar and aminos as well.
- Toss to coat well, cover slow cooker and cook on High for 6 hours.
- Divide ribs between plates and serve.
- Enjoy!

Nutrition:

- Calories - 300
- Fat - 6
- Carbs - 8
- Protein - 15

ZUCCHINI STEW

Preparation + Cooking time: 30 minutes
Serving: 3
Ingredients:

- 1 large zucchini, sliced into 1-inch thick slices
- 1 lb lamb loin, chopped into bite-sized pieces
- 4 garlic cloves, crushed
- 3 tbsp olive oil
- 1 cup purple cabbage, shredded
- 1 small chili pepper, finely chopped
- 2 cups beef stock
- Spices: 1 tsp salt
- ½ tsp chili powder
- 1 tsp oregano
- ¼ tsp dried thyme

Directions:

- Plug in the instant pot and press the "Saute" button. Heat up the oil and add garlic. Cook for one minute and then add the meat. Season with salt, chili powder,
- oregano, and thyme. Stir well and continue to cook for 5-6 minutes, stirring occasionally.
- Now add zucchini and give it a good stir.
- Stir-fry for 3 minutes.
- Pour in the stock and add chili pepper and cabbage. Seal the lid and set the steam release handle to the "Sealing" position.
- Press the "MANUAL" button and set the timer for 12 minutes on high pressure.
- When done, release the pressure naturally and open the lid.
- Optionally, top with Greek yogurt before serving.

Nutrition:

- Calories - 442
- Fat - 25.7g
- Carbs - 4.6g
- Protein - 46.2g

PORK SHOULDER RECIPE

Preparation + Cooking time: 40 minutes
Serving: 4
Ingredients:

- 2 -pounds pork shoulder roast
- 2 shallots; sliced
- 4 garlic cloves; crushed
- 3 tablespoon olive oil
- 3 tablespoon Dijon mustard
- 1 tablespoon fresh rosemary; finely chopped
- 1/2 teaspoon white pepper; freshly ground
- 1 teaspoon salt

Directions:

- Rinse well the meat and sprinkle with salt and pepper, Set aside.
- Take a round oven-safe bowl and coat with olive oil. Make a layer with shallots and sprinkle with garlic and fresh rosemary
- Place the meat on top and generously brush with Dijon mustard. Loosely cover with aluminum foil and set aside
- Plug in the instant pot and set the trivet in the inner pot. Pour in one cup of water and place the bowl on the trivet.
- Seal the lid and set the steam release handle to the "SEALING" position and press the "MANUAL" button.
- Set the timer for 25 minutes on high pressure
- When done; release the pressure naturally and open the lid. Remove the bowl from the pot and chill for a while.
- Serve and enjoy.

Nutrition:

- Calories - 430
- Fat - 19g
- Carbs - 2g
- Protein - 60.2g

SWEET CHILI SAUCE BRAISED PORK

Serving: 4
Preparation time: 5 minutes
Cooking time: 45 minutes
Ingredients:

- 1 tablespoon vegetable oil
- 1 onion, chopped
- 1-pound pork shoulder, cut into large chunks
- ½ cup white sugar
- ½ cup water
- 3 tablespoons sweet chili sauce
- 3 cloves of garlic, minced
- 1 tablespoon sesame oil
- 1 tablespoon fish sauce
- 1 tablespoon hoisin sauce
- 1 teaspoon ground ginger

Directions:

- Press the Saute button on the Instant Pot.
- Stir in the vegetable oil and saute the onion.
- Add in the pork shoulder. Stir for 3 minutes until the pork has turned golden.
- Pour in the rest of the ingredients.
- Close the lid and press the Meat/Stew button.
- Adjust the cooking time to 45 minutes.
- Do natural pressure release.

Nutrition:

- Calories - 457
- Carbs - 11.4g
- Protein - 30.7g
- Fat - 31.8g

FAJITAS

Serving: 4 (1 fajita per serving)
Ingredients:

- ¾ lb beef top sirloin steak, cut into thin strips
- 1 Tbsp lemon juice
- ¾ tsp ground cu minutes
- ¼ tsp chili powder
- ½ tsp seasoned salt
- ¼ tsp crushed red pepper flakes
- 1 medium onion, thinly sliced
- 1 Tbsp canola oil
- 1 small clove garlic, peeled, minced
- 1 medium bell pepper, cut into thin strips
- 4 mini whole wheat tortillas (5 inches each)
- Optional toppings: 1 small avocado, peeled, pitted, sliced
- ½ cup shredded cheddar cheese
- 1 jalapeno, deseed if desired, thinly sliced
- A handful fresh cilantro, chopped

Directions:

- Place a skillet over medium heat. Add oil and heat. When the oil is heated, add steak and cook until brown all over. Turn off the heat.
- Add garlic, lemon juice, chili powder, cumin, red pepper flakes and salt and mix well.
- Cover and cook for 2 hours on high or until meat is nearly cooked.
- Stir in the onion and red pepper.
- Cover and continue cooking until the meat is well cooked.
- Heat the tortillas following the instructions on the package.
- Place tortillas on a serving platter. Divide the beef and vegetables along the diameter of the tortillas.
- Place the optional toppings if desired and serve.

Nutrition:

- Calories - 220 (without optional toppings)

PINEAPPLE PORK

Preparation time: 8-10 minutes
Cooking time: 25 minutes
Serving: 2
Ingredients:

- 1 cup unsweetened pineapple juice
- ½ cup pineapple chunks
- ½ teaspoon nutmeg
- ½ teaspoon cinnamon
- 2 cloves
- ¼ cup chopped onion
- ½ teaspoon rosemary
- ½ pounds. pork tenderloin, sliced
- ½ cup tomato puree

Directions:

- Switch on the pot after placing it on a clean and dry platform.
- Open the pot lid and place the above-mentioned ingredients in the cooking pot area. Give the ingredients a little stir. Do not add the chunks.
- Close the pot by closing the top lid. Also, ensure to seal the valve.
- Press "MANUAL" cooking function and set cooking time to 25 minutes. It will start cooking after a few minutes. Let the pot mix cook under pressure until the timer reads zero.
- Press "Cancel" cooking function and press "Quick release" setting.
- Open the pot; add the chunks and serve warm. Enjoy it with your loved one!

Nutrition:

- Calories - 292
- Fat - 5g
- Carbs - 30g
- Protein - 31.5g

LAMB TAGINE

Preparation time: 20 minutes
Cooking time: 10 hours
Serving: 6
Ingredients:

- 2-pound lamb
- 2 oz fresh ginger
- 1 tablespoon minced garlic
- 1 teaspoon paprika
- 1 teaspoon turmeric
- 1 teaspoon onion powder
- 1 oz sugar
- 2 cups tomatoes, canned
- 1 tablespoon prune
- 1 tablespoon dried apricot
- 3 oz lemon
- ¼ teaspoon cinnamon
- ½ tablespoon honey
- 2 yellow onion
- 2 cups water

Directions:

- Chop the lamb roughly and put it in the slow cooker bowl.
- Peel the fresh ginger and grate it then add the grated fresh ginger into the slow cooker.
- Sprinkle the meat with the paprika, minced garlic, turmeric, onion powder, sugar, cinnamon, and honey.
- Chop the canned tomatoes, prunes, and dried apricots.
- Add them into the slow cooker as well. Peel the onions and chop them.
- Add the chopped onions in the slow cooker too. After this, slice the lemon and put it in the chopped onion.
- Add water and close the lid.
- Cook the lamb tagine for 10 hours on LOW. When the dish is cooked, let it cool slightly.
- Enjoy!

Nutrition:

- Calories - 462
- Fat - 25.8
- Carbs - 18.26
- Protein - 38

MAPLE GLAZED PORK RIBS

Serving: 6
Ingredients:

- ¼ cup soy sauce
- 2 tablespoons sugar free maple syrup

- 3 cloves garlic, crushed and minced
- 1 tablespoon fresh thyme
- 1 cup onion, sliced
- 1 cup butternut squash, cubed
- 1 cup green bell pepper, cubed
- 1 teaspoon salt
- 1 teaspoon black pepper
- 2 pounds pork ribs, cut into sections
- 1 cup chicken or beef stock

Directions:

- In a small bowl, combine the soy sauce, maple syrup, garlic, and thyme. Mix well.
- Place the onion, butternut squash, and green bell pepper in the bottom of a slow cooker.
- Season the vegetables with salt and black pepper.
- Baste the ribs with the sauce and place them in the slow cooker.
- Pour in the chicken or beef stock.
- Cover and cook on low for 10 hours.

Nutrition:

- Calories - 595.2
- Fat - 44.9 g
- Carbs - 8.2 g
- Protein - 38.3 g

SIMPLE TOMATO PORK CHOPS

Preparation + Cooking time: 40 minutes
Serving: 2
Ingredients:

- 2 pork chops, with bones
- 1 cup cherry tomatoes
- 1 green bell pepper, sliced
- 1 small onion, finely chopped
- 4 tbsp olive oil
- 1 cup beef broth
- Spices: ½ tsp salt
- ½ tsp white pepper, freshly ground
- ¼ tsp garlic powder

Directions:

- Place the meat in the pot and season with salt. Pour in the broth and seal the lid. Set the steam release handle to the "Sealing" position and press the "MANUAL" button.
- Set the timer for 15 minutes on high pressure. When done, release the pressure naturally and open the lid.
- Remove the meat from the pot and Set aside.
- Now, press the "Saute" button and grease the inner pot with olive oil. Heat up and add onions and peppers. Sprinkle with some more salt. Cook for 5-6 minutes and then add

cherry tomatoes. Pour in about ¼ cup of the broth and simmer for 10-12 minutes, stirring occasionally.

- Season with pepper and garlic powder. Optionally, add some red pepper flakes. Drizzle over pork chope and serve immediately.

Nutrition:

- Calories - 633
- Fat - 37g
- Carbs - 9.1g
- Protein - 63.6g

MOLE BEEF STEW

Serving: 4
Preparation time: 5 minutes
Cooking time: 45 minutes
Ingredients:

- 1 tablespoon olive oil
- 1 onion, chopped
- 3 cloves garlic, chopped
- 1 stalk celery, chopped
- 1 can plum tomatoes
- 1 cup vegetable stock
- ½ cup red wine
- 1-pound beef stew meat, cut into chunks
- 1 cup carrots, chopped
- ½ cup chocolate powder
- Salt and pepper

Directions:

- Press the Saute button on the Instant Pot.
- Heat the oil and saute the onion and garlic.
- Add in the beef stew meat and stir for another 3 minutes until lightly brown.
- Stir in the rest of the ingredients. Mix well to combine.
- Close the lid and press the Meat/Stew button.
- Adjust the cooking time to 40 minutes.
- Do natural pressure release.

Nutrition:

- Calories - 668
- Carbs - 15.6g
- Protein - 38.2g
- Fat - 15.8 g

PORK POZOLE

Preparation time: 10 minutes

Cooking time: 4.5 hours
Serving: 6
Ingredients:

- 1 ½ pound pork loin, chopped
- 1 cup edamame beans
- 1 teaspoon minced garlic
- 1 white onion, chopped
- 1 teaspoon ground cu minutes
- 1 teaspoon ground coriander
- 1 teaspoon salt
- 1 teaspoon paprika
- ½ teaspoon peppercorns
- 1 cup chicken stock
- 1/3 cup tomato sauce

Directions:

- Mix up together chicken stock, tomato sauce, peppercorns, paprika, salt, ground coriander, and cumin in the bowl and pour the mixture in the crockpot.
- Add chopped pork loin edamame beans, minced garlic, and chopped onion.
- Then close the lid and cook Pork Pozole for 4.5 hours on High.

Nutrition:

- Calories - 322
- Fat - 17.4
- Carbs - 5.7
- Protein - 34.5

KETO SAMBAR

Preparation + Cooking time: 55 minutes
Serving: 6
Ingredients:

- 2 lbs pork chops, cut into bite-sized pieces
- 2 small tomatoes, chopped
- 2 cups cauliflower, chopped into florets
- 1 cup eggplant, chopped into chunks
- 1 large onion, finely chopped
- 2 chili peppers, whole
- 3 garlic cloves, crushed
- 4 tbsp ghee
- 4 cups vegetable stock
- 1 cup coconut milk
- Spices: 2 tsp sambar powder
- 1 tbsp jiggery powder
- 2 tsp salt
- 1 tsp black pepper
- ¼ cup fresh parsley, finely chopped

- 3 tsp turmeric powder
- 2 tbsp chili powder
- 3 tbsp brown mustard seeds

Directions:

- Place vegetables in a large colander and rinse well.
- Drain and set aside.
- Cut the meat into bite-sized pieces. Place in a deep bowl and sprinkle with salt and pepper.
- Set aside.
- Plug in the instant pot and grease the inner pot with ghee. Press the "Saute" button and add mustard seeds. Cook for 1 minute and then add onions, garlic, and chili pepper.
- Stir well and cook for 3-4 minutes.
- Now add cauliflower and eggplant. Pour in some of the stock and bring it to a boil.
- Simmer for 5 minutes.
- Finally, add the remaining ingredients and stir well. Seal the lid and set the steam release handle to the "Sealing" position and press the "MANUAL" button.
- Set the timer for 35 minutes on high pressure.
- When done, release the pressure naturally and optionally sprinkle with some more fresh parsley.
- Serve immediately.

Nutrition:

- Calories - 600
- Fat - 46.3g
- Carbs - 4.8g
- Protein - 36.1g
-

GROUND PORK WITH EGGS

Preparation + Cooking time: 20 minutes
Serving: 4
Ingredients:

- 7 oz ground pork
- 2 bacon slices, chopped
- 1 onion, finely chopped
- 4 large eggs
- 1 garlic clove, crushed
- 3 tbsp butter
- Spices: ½ tsp salt
- ½ tsp pepper, freshly ground

Directions:

- Grease the bottom of the pot with butter and press the "Saute" button.
- Add onions and briefly cook - for 2-3 minutes.
- Now add pork, bacon, and garlic. Season with salt and pepper.

- Continue to cook for 5 minutes.
- Finally, crack the eggs and cook for 2-3 minutes. Press the "Cancel" button and serve immediately.

Nutrition:

- Calories - 282
- Fat - 19.4g
- Carbs - 2.8g
- Protein - 23.2g

JUICY LAMB CHOPS

Serving: 4-6
Ingredients:

- 2 pounds lamb chops, cut in 1 ½ inch chops
- 2 tablespoons vegetable oil
- 2 tablespoons black pepper, ground
- 2 tablespoons black pepper, whole
- ½ teaspoon salt
- ¼ cup onion, chopped
- ¼ cup garlic, minced
- 2 tablespoons oregano, ground
- 2 tablespoons mustard seeds, ground
- 1 cup vegetable or chicken broth
- ½ cup gluten-free soy sauce

Directions:

- Rub lamb with salt and ground pepper. Arrange in the slow cooker.
- Combine the oil, whole black pepper, onion, garlic, oregano, mustard seeds, broth and soy sauce, and add.
- Cook for 12 hours on a low setting.
- Serve with steamed rice and salad.

Nutrition:

- Calories - 627
- Fat - 32.7 g
- Carbs - 26.1 g
- Protein - 127.6 g

CITRUS LAMB

Preparation + Cooking time: 50 minutes
Serving: 4
Ingredients:

- 1 lb lamb tenderloin, chopped into bite-sized pieces
- 1 cup cherry tomatoes, chopped

- 3 tbsp butter
- 1 cup coconut milk, full-fat
- 2 cups chicken broth
- 2 large onions, finely chopped
- 1 cup cilantro, finely chopped
- 2 tbsp lemon juice
- 2 tbsp apple cider
- Spices: 1 tsp salt
- 3 tbsp chili powder
- 2 tsp garam masala
- 2 tsp turmeric powder
- 1 tbsp cumin powder

Directions:

- Rinse the meat under cold running water and pat dry with some kitchen paper. Generously sprinkle with salt and pepper and place in the instant pot.
- Press the "Saute" button and cook for 4-5 minutes, stirring occasionally.
- Now add the remaining ingredients and season with spices. Stir well and seal the lid.
- Set the steam release handle to the "Sealing" position and press the "MANUAL" button.
- Set the timer for 15 minutes on high pressure.
- When you hear the cooker's end signal, press the "Cancel" button and release the pressure naturally. Carefully open the lid and chill for a while before serving.

Nutrition:

- Calories - 224
- Fat - 7.4g
- Carbs - 6.6g
- Protein - 28.8g

VIETNAMESE BEEF BO KHO

Serving: 4
Preparation time: 3 minutes
Cooking time: 45 minutes
Ingredients:

- 1 onion, chopped
- 1-pound beef chuck stew meat, cut into chunks
- 2 tablespoons tomato paste
- 2 whole star anise
- 1 lemongrass stalk
- 1 tablespoon ginger, grated
- 1 tablespoon garlic, minced
- 1 ½ cups water
- ½ cups coconut water
- ½ teaspoon curry powder

Directions:

- Place all ingredients in the Instant Pot.
- Close the lid and press the Meat/Stew button.
- Adjust the cooking time to 45 minutes.
- Do natural pressure release.

Nutrition:

- Calories - 175
- Carbs - 8g
- Protein - 15g
- Fat - 9g

THYME LAMB

Preparation + Cooking time: 1 hour 15 minutes
Serving: 4
Ingredients:

- 2 lbs lamb shoulder
- 1 cup fresh thyme, chopped
- 1 tbsp ground black pepper
- 1 tsp paprika
- 1 tsp oregano
- ¼ cup rice wine
- 1 tbsp turmeric
- 1 tsp sugar
- ¼ cup chicken stock
- 1 tbsp olive oil
- ½ cup water
- 4 tbsp butter

Directions:

- In a large bowl, combine the thyme, black pepper, paprika, oregano, rice wine, turmeric, sugar and chicken stock. Mix well.
- Rub all sides of the lamb shoulder with the spice mix.
- Select the SAUTe setting on the Instant Pot and heat the oil.
- Add the lamb and brown for 5 minutes on both sides.
- Add the remaining spice mixture, water and butter to the pot, stir.
- Once the butter is melted, press the CANCEL key to stop the SAUTe function.
- Close and lock the lid. Select MANUAL and cook at HIGH pressure for 45 minutes.
- When the timer goes off, let the pressure
- Release Naturally for 10 minutes, then release any remaining steam manually. Open the lid.
- If desired, broil in the oven for 8-10 minutes for a browned top.
- Serve.

PENANG BEEF CURRY

Serving: 8
Ingredients:

- 1 pound beef, cubed
- 1 cup coconut cream
- 1 onion, chopped
- 1 teaspoon ground cardamom
- 1 teaspoon Chinese five-spice
- ½ teaspoon chili powder
- 1 teaspoon ground cu minutes
- 1 teaspoon turmeric
- 4 cloves
- 2 teaspoons coriander
- ½ teaspoon salt

Directions:

- Put the coconut cream and all the spices into the slow cooker. Mix until well combined.
- Add the chopped onion and cubed beef.
- Cook for about 8-9 hours on low.
- Top with some fresh coriander.

Nutrition:

- Calories - 256
- Fat - 14 g
- Carbs - 2 g
- Protein - 29 g

GLAZED PEPPER PORK

Preparation time: 5-8 minutes
Cooking time: 65-70 minutes
Serving: 3-4
Ingredients:

- 1 teaspoon dried sage
- ½ teaspoon black pepper
- 2 pounds boneless pork loin
- 1 garlic clove, minced
- ½ cup beef broth
- Glaze: ½ cup coconut sugar
- ¼ cup balsamic vinegar
- 1 tablespoon arrowroot
- ½ cup water
- 2 tablespoon coconut aminos

Directions:

- Mix the sage, garlic, and pepper in a small bowl. Rub this mixture into the meat.
- Switch on your instant pot after placing it on a clean and dry kitchen platform.

- Open the pot lid and slowly start adding the broth to the pot. Arrange the trivet inside it; arrange the meat over the trivet.
- Close the pot by closing the top lid. Also, ensure to seal the valve.
- Press "MANUAL" cooking function and set cooking time to 60 minutes. It will start cooking after a few minutes. Let the pot mix cook under pressure until the timer reads zero.
- Turn off and press "Cancel" cooking function. Allow the inside pressure to release naturally; it will take 8-10 minutes to release all inside pressure.
- Open the pot.
- Mix the glaze ingredients in a bowl and add in your Instant Pot. Cook for 2 minutes on saute.
- Shred the meat and drizzle the glaze over. Serve warm!

Nutrition:

- Calories - 562
- Fat - 22.5g
- Carbs - 27g
- Protein - 61.5g

SNACKS

BACON TURKEY MEATBALLS

Preparation time: 15 minutes
Cooking time: 4 hours
Serving: 4
Ingredients:

- 1 cup ground turkey
- 4 bacon slices
- 1 teaspoon ground black pepper
- 1 tablespoon coconut flour
- ½ teaspoon salt
- 1/3 cup coconut cream

Directions:

- Mix up together ground turkey with ground black pepper, coconut flour, and salt.
- Make the small meatballs from the turkey mixture.
- Coat every meatball in the sliced bacon and secure with a toothpick.
- Put the meatballs in the crockpot. Add coconut cream.
- Close the crockpot lid and cook meatballs for 4 hours on High.

Nutrition:

- Calories - 319
- Fat - 22
- Carbs - 3
- Protein - 30.4

CHICKEN DIP

Preparation time: 10 minutes
Cooking time: 3 hours and 30 minutes
Serving: 10
Ingredients:

- 1 pound chicken breast, skinless, boneless and sliced
- 3 tablespoons sriracha sauce
- ¼ cup chicken stock
- 2 tablespoons stevia
- 1 teaspoon hot sauce
- 8 ounces coconut cream

Directions:

- In your slow cooker, mix chicken with sriracha sauce, stock, stevia and hot sauce, stir, cover and cook on High for 3 hours.
- Shred meat, return to pot, also add coconut cream, cover and cook on High for 30 minutes more.
- Divide into bowls and serve as a party dip.
- Enjoy!

Nutrition:

- Calories - 231
- Fat - 3
- Carbs - 10
- Protein - 3

MIXED SEEDS BARS

Preparation time: 10 minutes
Cooking time: 45 minutes
Serving: 6
Ingredients:

- 1 oz dark chocolate
- 2 tablespoons peanut butter
- 1 tablespoon sunflower seeds
- 2 tablespoons pumpkin seeds
- 2 tablespoons walnuts, chopped
- 1 tablespoon chia seeds, dried
- 1 tablespoon coconut flakes

Directions:

- Put the dark chocolate and peanut butter in the crockpot. Close the lid and cook the ingredients on High for 15 minutes.
- After this, add sunflower seeds, pumpkin seeds, walnuts, and chia seeds.
- Add coconut flakes and stir the mixture carefully with the help of the spatula.

- Close the lid and cook the mixture for 30 minutes on High.
- Then line the tray with baking paper and Flatten it well and let it cool.
- Then brake the seeds crust into the bars.

Nutrition:

- Calories - 99
- Fat - 7.3
- Carbs - 5.2
- Protein - 2.8

CARAMELIZED ONION APPETIZER

Preparation time: 10 minutes
Cooking time: 6 hours
Serving: 32
Ingredients:

- 1 apple, peeled, cored and chopped
- 2 cups sweet onions, sliced
- 2 tablespoons ghee
- ½ cup cranberries
- ¼ cup balsamic vinegar
- 1 tablespoon stevia
- ½ teaspoon orange zest, grated
- 7 ounces cashew cheese, shredded

Directions:

- In your slow cooker, mix apples with cranberries, onions, ghee, vinegar, stevia and orange zest, stir, cover and cook on Low for 6 hours.
- Divide into bowls, sprinkle cashew cheese on to and serve as an appetizer.
- Enjoy!

Nutrition:

- Calories - 32
- Fat - 2
- Carbs - 3
- Protein - 4

GRAIN-FREE GRANOLA

Serving: 2
Preparation time: 5 minutes
Cooking time: 6 hours
Ingredients:

- 1/2 cup shredded coconut, unsweetened
- 1/4 cup seeds and nuts (can be a mixture of sunflower and pumpkin seeds with almond
- 1 tsp sweetener

- 1 tbsp unsweetened coco powder
- 1 tbsp cocoa nibs

Directions:

- Mix all ingredients in the crockpot. Add 1 tsp of oil for extra moisture.
- Cover and cook for 6 hours on low.

Nutrition:

- Calories - 277
- Fat - 26 g
- Carbs - 2.9 g
- Protein - 4.8 g

SALTY PEANUT BOMBS

Preparation time: 15 minutes
Cooking time: 6 hours
Serving: 9
Ingredients:

- 1 cup peanut
- ½ cup flour
- 1 egg
- 1 teaspoon butter
- 1 teaspoon salt
- 1 teaspoon turmeric
- 4 tablespoons milk
- ¼ teaspoon nutmeg

Directions:

- Put the peanuts in a blender and blend them well. Combine the blended peanuts with the flour. Crack the egg into the bowl and whisk.
- Add salt, turmeric, milk, and nutmeg. Stir gently.
- Combine the flour mixture and egg mixture together. Knead into a smooth dough. Toss the butter in the slow cooker bowl and melt on HIGH for 10 minutes.
- After this, make small balls from the dough and put them in the slow cooker. Close the lid and cook the bombs on SLOW for 6 hours.
- Check if the bombs are cooked and remove them from the slow cooker. Put them on paper towel and chill well. Enjoy!

Nutrition:

- Calories - 215
- Fat - 12.7
- Carbs - 17.4
- Protein - 10

SNAP BEANS PAPRIKA DIP

Preparation time: 15 minutes
Cooking time: 7 hours
Serving: 5
Ingredients:

- 1 cup snap beans
- 1 green bell pepper, chopped
- 1 teaspoon smoked paprika
- ½ teaspoon salt
- ½ teaspoon chili pepper
- 1/3 cup heavy cream
- ½ teaspoon ground nutmeg

Directions:

- Put snap beans, bell pepper, smoked paprika, salt, chili pepper, and ground nutmeg in the crockpot.
- Add heavy cream and stir the ingredients carefully.
- Close the crockpot lid and cook the mixture for 7 hours on Low.
- After this, use the hand blender or fork to mash the mixture until smooth.
- Chill the cooked dip well before serving.

Nutrition:

- Calories - 42
- Fat - 3.2
- Carbs - 3.3
- Protein - 0.8

PARSLEY SHRIMP BOWLS

Preparation time: 5 minutes
Cooking time: 1 hour and 30 minutes
Serving: 4
Ingredients:

- 1 cup vegetable stock
- 1 pound shrimp, peeled and deveined
- Juice of 1 lime
- 3 tablespoons olive oil
- Salt and black pepper to the taste
- 4 tablespoons parsley, chopped

Directions:

- In your slow cooker, combine all the ingredients except the parsley. Cover and cook on low for 1 hour and 30 minutes.
- Add the parsley, mix, divide into bowls and serve as an appetizer.

Nutrition:

- Calories - 231
- Fat - 13
- Carbs - 3,4
- Protein - 26

EASY CHEESECAKE

Serving: 2
Preparation time: 15 minutes
Cooking time: 2 hours 30 minutes
Ingredients:

- 24 oz cream cheese
- 3 eggs
- 1 cup gluten-free sweetener
- ½ tbsp vanilla

Directions:

- Mix all ingredients thoroughly using a mixer in a bowl.
- Pour 2 to 3 cups of water in the crockpot and place the bowl inside.
- Cover and cook for 2 hours and 30 minutes on high.

Nutrition:

- Calories - 207
- Fat - 16.1 g
- Carbs - 5.7 g
- Protein - 7.8 g
- Serving suggestions: Serve with any low-sugar fruit sauce or sliced fruits.

SPECIAL MUSHROOMS APPETIZER

Preparation time: 10 minutes
Cooking time: 8 hours
Serving: 8
Ingredients:

- 1 shallot, chopped
- 2 garlic cloves, minced
- 2 tablespoons parsley, chopped
- 1 and ½ pounds button mushrooms
- ½ cup chicken stock
- ½ cup coconut cream
- A pinch of salt and black pepper

Directions:

- In your slow cooker, mix shallot with garlic, parsley, stock, cream, salt and pepper and whisk well.
- Add mushrooms, cover and cook on Low for 8 hours.

- Arrange mushrooms on a platter and serve them as an appetizer.
- Enjoy!

Nutrition:

- Calories - 130
- Fat - 3
- Carbs - 7
- Protein - 3

MEATBALLS APPETIZER

Preparation time: 10 minutes
Cooking time: 2 hours and 30 minutes
Serving: 6
Ingredients:

- 1 egg
- 1 pound chicken, ground
- ½ teaspoon garlic powder
- ½ teaspoon onion powder
- 2 green onions, chopped
- A pinch of salt and black pepper
- ¾ cup Paleo buffalo sauce

Directions:

- In a bowl, mix chicken with egg, onion powder, garlic powder, green onions, salt and pepper and stir well.
- Shape meatballs, add them to your slow cooker, also add buffalo sauce, cover and cook on Low for 2 hours and 30 minutes.
- Arrange meatballs on a platter and serve them with the sauce on the side.
- Enjoy!

Nutrition:

- Calories - 221
- Fat - 4
- Carbs - 8
- Protein - 6

BLUEBERRY LEMON CUSTARD CAKE

Serving: 2
Preparation time: 15 minutes
Cooking time: 3 hours
Ingredients:

- 2 eggs
- 1/4 cup coconut flour
- 1/8 cup lemon juice

- 1/8 cup sweetener
- 1/4 cup fresh blueberries

Directions:

- Mix all ingredients, except blueberries, thoroughly using a mixer in a bowl.
- Pour the mixture in the crockpot.
- Cover and cook for 3 hours on high.

Nutrition:

- al Value:
- Calories - 140
- Fat - 9.2 g
- Carbs - 5.1 g
- Protein - 3.9 g

CHICKEN WINGS

Preparation time: 10 minutes
Cooking time: 4 hours
Serving: 4
Ingredients:

- ¼ cup coconut aminos
- ¼ cup balsamic vinegar
- 2 garlic cloves, minced
- 2 tablespoon stevia
- 1 teaspoon sriracha sauce
- 3 tablespoons lime juice
- Zest from 1 lime, grated
- 1 teaspoon ginger powder
- 2 teaspoons sesame seeds
- 2 pounds chicken wings
- 2 tablespoons chives, chopped

Directions:

- In your slow cooker, mix aminos with vinegar, garlic, stevia, sriracha, lime juice, lime zest and ginger and stir well.
- Add chicken wings, toss well, cover and cook on High for 4 hours.
- Arrange chicken wings on a platter, sprinkle chives and sesame seeds on top and serve as a casual appetizer.
- Enjoy!

Nutrition:

- Calories - 212
- Fat - 3
- Carbs - 12
- Protein - 3

CRUSTLESS BEEF PIZZA

Serving: 2
Preparation time: 15 minutes
Cooking time: 4 hours
Ingredients:

- 3/4 cup pizza sauce
- 1 lb ground beef, browned
- 1 cup mozzarella cheese
- pizza toppings of your choice (pepperoni, mushrooms, peppers, etc.

Directions:

- Mix the ground beef and mozzarella in the crockpot then spread evenly across the bottom.
- Top it with pizza sauce then put the desired toppings.
- Cover and cook for 4 hours on low.

Nutrition:

- Calories - 178
- Fat - 9.8 g
- Carbs - 4/8 g
- Protein - 10.4 g

MUSTARD GREENS DIP

Preparation time: 5 minutes
Cooking time: 2 hours
Serving: 4
Ingredients:

- 1 pound mustard greens, chopped
- ½ cup vegetable stock
- 2 tablespoons fresh chopped basil
- 2 spring onions, chopped
- 1 cup coconut cream
- A pinch of salt and black pepper

Directions:

- In your slow cooker, combine all the ingredients, cover and cook on low for 2 hours.
- Blend using an immersion blender, divide into bowls and serve cold.

Nutrition:

- Calories - 171
- Fat - 14,8
- Carbs - 9,7
- Protein - 4,6

TENDER JALAPENO PEPPERS

Preparation time: 15 minutes
Cooking time: 1.5 hour
Serving: 8
Ingredients:

- 8 jalapeno pepper
- 1 tablespoon cream cheese
- ½ cup Cheddar cheese, shredded
- ¼ cup crushed tomatoes
- 1 teaspoon butter

Directions:

- Cut the ends of jalapeno peppers and remove seeds.
- Then mix up together shredded Cheddar cheese and cream cheese.
- Fill the jalapenos with cheese mixture and place in the crockpot.
- Add butter and crushed tomatoes.
- Close the crockpot lid and cook jalapeno peppers for 1.5 hours on High.

Nutrition:

- Calories - 44
- Fat - 3.4
- Carbs - 1.6
- Protein - 2.2

KIDS FAVORITE PECANS

Preparation + Cooking time: 41 minutes
Serving: 30
Ingredients:

- For Pecans: 1 tsp butter
- 4 cups raw pecans
- ¼ cup Erythritol
- ½ tsp ground cinnamon
- Pinch of sea salt
- ½ cup filtered water
- For Chocolate coating: 2 tbsp. Erythritol
- 1 tsp ground cinnamon
- 1 (20-ounce) block 85% dark chocolate

Directions:

- Place the butter in the Instant Pot and select "Saute". Then, add all ingredients except water and cook for about 5 minutes, stirring frequently.
- Select the "Cancel" and stir in water.
- Secure the lid and place the pressure valve to "Seal" position.
- Select "MANUAL" and cook under "High Pressure" for about 10 minutes.

- Meanwhile, preheat the oven to 350 degrees F.
- Select the "Cancel" and carefully do a "Natural" release for about 10 minutes and then do a "Quick" release.
- Remove the lid and Bake for about 5 minutes.
- Remove from oven and keep aside to cool.
- For coating: dust the pecans with the Erythritol and cinnamon.
- In a heatproof bowl, place chocolate.
- In the bottom of Instant Pot, arrange a steamer trivet and pour 1 cup of water.
- Place the bowl on top of trivet and select "Saute". Cook for about 5-6 minutes or until melted completely.
- Select the "Cancel" and Add pecans and coat well.
- Remove from bowl and keep aside to cool completely before serving.

Nutrition:

- Calories - 129
- Fat - 8.3g
- Carbs - 0.46g
- Protein - 1.7g

CHEESE HOT DIP

Preparation time: 10 minutes
Cooking time: 4 hours
Serving: 5
Ingredients:

- 1 cup Italian sausages, crumbled
- 1 tablespoon chives, chopped
- 1 teaspoon fresh basil, chopped
- 1 cup Cheddar cheese, shredded
- 1 cup Mozzarella cheese, shredded
- ¼ cup heavy cream

Directions:

- Put Italian sausages in the skillet and roast them for 5 minutes over the medium heat.
- Then Add heavy cream, fresh basil, and chives.
- Then add Mozzarella and Cheddar cheese.
- Close the lid and cook dip for 4 hours on Low.

Nutrition:

- Calories - 284
- Fat - 24.9
- Carbs - 1
- Protein - 13.8

CHILI CHICKEN SPREAD

Preparation time: 5 minutes

Cooking time: 3 hours and 5 minutes
Serving: 8
Ingredients:

- 1 yellow onion, chopped
- 2 teaspoons olive oil
- 3 cups chicken breasts, skinless, boneless, cooked and shredded
- 12 ounces coconut cream
- ½ cup chili sauce
- 2 tablespoons fresh chopped chives

Directions:

- Heat up a pan with the oil over medium-high heat, add the onion, stir, cook for 5 minutes and Add all the remaining ingredients, toss, cover and cook on low for 3 hours.
- Divide into bowls and serve.

Nutrition:

- Calories - 215
- Fat - 15,3
- Carbs - 3,9
- Protein - 16,4

BEEF BITES

Preparation time: 5 minutes
Cooking time: 8 hours
Serving: 10
Ingredients:

- 2 pounds beef, cubed
- 1 red chili pepper, chopped
- 1/5 cup tomato sauce

Directions:

- In your slow cooker, combine all the ingredients, cover and cook on low for 8 hours.
- Divide into bowls and serve warm.

Nutrition:

- Calories - 170
- Fat - 5,7
- Carbs - 0,3
- Protein - 27,6

DESSERTS

SPECIAL DESSERT

Preparation time: 10 minutes
Cooking time: 1 hour and 30 minutes
Serving: 8
Ingredients:

- 1/3 cup coconut flour
- ½ teaspoon baking soda
- 3 eggs
- 5 tablespoons coconut oil
- 2 tablespoons honey
- For the topping: 4 tablespoons coconut oil, melted
- 1 tablespoon cinnamon powder
- 1 cup honey

Directions:

- In a bowl, mix flour with baking soda, eggs, 5 tablespoons coconut oil and 2 tablespoons honey, stir well until you obtain a dough and shape 8 balls out of it.
- In a bowl, mix 4 tablespoons melted oil with cinnamon and 1 cup honey and whisk really well.
- Dip balls into this mix and arrange them in your slow cooker.
- Cover and cook on Low for 1 hour and 30 minutes.
- Leave this Paleo dessert to cool down before serving it.
- Enjoy!

Nutrition:

- Calories - 230
- Fat - 2
- Carbs - 6
- Protein - 7

RUTABAGA SWEET PIE

Preparation time: 20 minutes
Cooking time: 4.5 hours
Serving: 6
Ingredients:

- 1 cup almond flour
- ¾ cup butter, softened
- 1 tablespoon Erythritol
- 1 teaspoon liquid stevia
- 1 teaspoon ground cinnamon
- ½ teaspoon vanilla extract
- 1 cup rutabaga, chopped
- 1 tablespoon coconut oil
- Cooking spray

Directions:

- For the pie crust: mix up together almond flour, butter, and knead the soft dough.
- Then cut the dough into 2 parts.
- Spray the crockpot bottom with cooking spray from inside.
- Roll up first dough part with the help of the rolling pin and place it in the crockpot.
- Then mix up together rutabaga with vanilla extract, coconut oil, and ground cinnamon.
- Sprinkle it with Erythritol and liquid stevia.
- Then roll up the second dough part and cover the rutabaga.
- Close the crockpot lid and cook the pie for 4.5 hours on Low.
- When the pie is cooked, chill it well and only them cut into the pieces.

Nutrition:

- Calories - 260
- Fat - 27.7
- Carbs - 5.8
- Protein - 1.5

ALMOND CHOCOLATE BARS

Preparation time: 10 minutes
Cooking time: 2 hours and 30 minutes
Serving: 12
Ingredients:

- 1 egg white
- ¼ cup coconut oil, melted
- 1 cup coconut sugar
- ½ teaspoon vanilla extract
- 1 teaspoon baking powder
- 1 and ½ cups almond meal
- ½ cup dark chocolate chips

Directions:

- In a bowl, mix the oil with sugar, vanilla extract, egg white, baking powder and almond flour and whisk well
- Fold in chocolate chips and stir gently.
- Line your slow cooker with parchment paper, grease it, add cookie mix, press on the bottom, cover and cook on low for 2 hours and 30 minutes.
- Take cookie sheet out of the slow cooker, cut into medium bars and serve.
- Enjoy!

Nutrition:

- Calories - 200
- Fat - 2
- Carbs - 13
- Protein - 6

EASY ALMOND BROWNIES

Preparation + Cooking time: 40 minutes
Serving: 6
Ingredients:

- 2 large eggs
- ¾ cup swerve
- ½ cup almond flour
- ½ cup almonds, finely chopped
- 3 tsp baking powder
- ¼ cup coconut flour
- ½ cup whole milk
- ½ cup oil
- Topping: ¾ cup milk
- ¾ cup swerve
- 2 oz unsweetened dark chocolate
- 4 tbsp butter

Directions:

- In a large mixing bowl, combine together almond flour, coconut flour, baking powder, and swerve. Mix well and add eggs, one at the time, beating constantly with a paddle attachment on.
- Now pour in the milk and oil. Continue to beat for 2-3 minutes, or until completely incporporated.
- Lightly grease a small baking pan with some oil and line with some parchment paper.
- Dust with unsweetened cocoa powder.
- Pour the mixture into the prepared baking pan and loosely cover with aluminum foil.
- Plug in the instant pot and set the trivet at the bottom of the inner pot. Pour in one cup of water and place the pan on top.
- Seal the lid and set the steam release handle. Press the "MANUAL" button and set the timer for 25 minutes on high pressure.
- When done, perform a quick pressure relase and open the lid. Remove the pan from the pot and chill for a while.
- Now press the "Saute" button and melt the butter. Stir in the butter and chocolate. Pour in the milk and bring it to a boil.
- Cook until all the chocolate has melted.
- Pour the mixture over brownies and cool completely before slicing.

Nutrition:

- Calories - 470
- Fat - 45.8g
- Carbs - 5.8g
- Protein - 6.7g

PINEAPPLE BREAD PUDDING

Serving: 6
Ingredients:

- 1 cup pineapple, chopped into bite-sized chunks

- 3 tablespoons butter, melted
- 1 ½ cup milk
- ¼ cup condensed milk
- ¼ cup brown sugar
- 1 tablespoon lemon juice
- 8 thick egg bread slices, cut into cubes
- 4 large eggs
- 1 teaspoon cinnamon

Directions:

- In the slow cooker, place butter, milk, condensed milk and brown sugar. Whip the eggs and place in the bottom layer too.
- Layer in the bread slices then cook for 2 hours.
- Add the pineapples, lemon juice, and cinnamon.
- Cook for 4 hours on low.
- Slice into desired sizes.

Nutrition:

- Calories - 547
- Fat - 17.2 g
- Carbs - 86.5 g
- Protein - 13.3 g

ZUCCHINI CAKE

Preparation time: 10 minutes
Cooking time: 4 hours
Serving: 6
Ingredients:

- 1 cup natural applesauce
- 3 eggs, whisked
- 1 tablespoon vanilla extract
- 4 tablespoons stevia
- 2 cups zucchini, grated
- 2 and ½ cups coconut flour
- ½ cup baking cocoa powder
- 1 teaspoon baking soda
- ¼ teaspoon baking powder
- 1 teaspoon cinnamon powder
- Cooking spray

Directions:

- Grease your slow with cooking spray, add zucchini, sugar, vanilla, eggs, applesauce, flour, cocoa powder, baking soda, baking powder and cinnamon, whisk, cook on High for 4 hours, cool down, slice and serve.
- Enjoy!

Nutrition:

- Calories - 171
- Fat - 4
- Carbs - 10
- Protein - 3

EASY KETO FUDGE

Preparation time: 20 minutes
Cooking time: 40 minutes
Serving: 8
Ingredients:

- 2 tablespoons coconut cream
- 2 tablespoons ricotta cheese
- 1 teaspoon vanilla extract
- 1 teaspoon Erythritol
- 1/3 cup sugar-free chocolate chips
- 1 teaspoon butter

Directions:

- Put coconut cream and ricotta cheese in the crockpot.
- Add vanilla extract, Erythritol, chocolate chips, and butter.
- Mix up the fudge mixture well.
- Cook it for 40 minutes on High.
- Meanwhile, line the baking tray with baking paper.
- Stir the melted chocolate chip mixture and Cover it with the second sheet of baking paper.
- With the help of the rolling pin, roll up the fudge into the square.
- Cool it in the fridge for 10 minutes.
- Then discard the baking paper and cut fudge into the serving squares.
- Store dessert in the cool place.

Nutrition:

- Calories - 56
- Fat - 3.5
- Carbs - 7
- Protein - 0.9

VANILLA AND STRAWBERRY CHEESECAKE

Cooking time: 6 hours
Serving: 8

- Ingredients for base: Butter - 2 ounces, melted
- Ground hazelnuts - 1 cup
- Desiccated coconut - ½ cup
- Vanilla extract - 2 tsp.

- Cinnamon - 1 tsp.
- Filling
- Cream cheese - 2 cups
- Eggs - 2, lightly beaten
- Sour cream - 1 cup
- Vanilla extract - 2 tsp.
- Large strawberries - 8, chopped
- Method
- Prepare the base: in a bowl, combine the hazelnuts, melted butter, coconut, vanilla, and cinnamon.
- Press the base into a greased dish.
- In a bowl, place the eggs, cream cheese, sour cream, and vanilla extract.
- Beat with a hand mixture until thick and combined.
- Fold the strawberries through the cream cheese mixture.
- Pour the cream cheese mixture into the dish, on top of the base, spread until smooth.
- Place the dish into the Crock-Pot and add enough hot water around the dish so that it comes halfway up the sides of the dish.
- Place the lid onto the pot and cook on low for 6 hours or until just set, but still wobbly.
- Cool and serve.

Nutrition:

- Calories - 516
- Fat - 50.3g
- Carbs - 10.3g
- Protein - 9.5g

FRAGRANT CINNAMON ROLL

Preparation time: 15 minutes
Cooking time: 3.5 hours
Serving: 6
Ingredients:

- 1 teaspoon baking powder
- 1 cup almond flour
- 1 tablespoon ground cinnamon
- 2 tablespoons Erythritol
- 1/3 cup coconut oil
- 1 teaspoon vanilla extract
- 1 egg, beaten
- ¾ cup cream cheese

Directions:

- Make the cinnamon roll dough: mix up together baking powder, almond flour, coconut oil, vanilla extract, and beaten egg.
- Knead the soft dough. Add more almond flour if needed.
- Mix up together ground cinnamon with Erythritol.
- Roll up the dough with the help of the rolling pin.
- Spread the surface of the dough with ground cinnamon mixture and roll it into the log.

- Cut the log into 6 buns and secure the edges of every bun.
- Line the crockpot with baking paper.
- Place the buns in the crockpot and close the lid.
- Cook the cinnamon roll for 3.5 hours on High.
- Check if the rolls are cooked with the help of the toothpick - if it is dry, the buns are cooked.
- Chill the dessert well and then remove from the crockpot in the serving plate.

Nutrition:

- Calories - 248
- Fat - 25.3
- Carbs - 8.2
- Protein - 4.2

HOT FUDGE SUNDAE CAKE

Serving: 12
Preparation time: 10 minutes
Cooking time: 30 minutes
Ingredients:

- 1 ¾ cups packed brown sugar, divided
- 1 cup whole wheat flour
- 5 tablespoons baking cocoa, divided
- 2 teaspoons baking powder
- ½ teaspoon salt
- 2 tablespoons butter, melted
- ½ cup milk
- ½ teaspoon vanilla extract
- 1/8 teaspoon almond extract
- ½ cup boiling water
- 4 teaspoon instant coffee granules

Directions:

- Place a steamer in the Instant Pot and pour a cup of water.
- In a bowl, mix all the ingredients until well combined.
- Pour the batter into a dish that will fit inside the Instant Pot.
- Put aluminum foil on top.
- Place on the steamer and close the lid.
- Press the Manual button and adjust the cooking time for 30 minutes.
- Do natural pressure release.

Nutrition:

- Calories - 255
- Carbs - 48g
- Protein - 3g
- Fat - 7g

VANILLA CREAM

Preparation + Cooking time: 25 minutes
Serving: 4
Ingredients:

- 8 large eggs
- ¾ cup unsweetened almond milk
- 1 ½ cup heavy cream
- 1 tsp vanilla extract
- 1 vanilla bean
- 4 tbsp. swerve

Directions:

- Cut the vanilla bean lengthwise and scrape out the seeds. Place in a mixing bowl along with the remaining ingredients.
- With a whisking attachment on, beat the mixture for 2 minutes on high speed and Tightly wrap with aluminum foil and set aside.
- Plug in your instant pot and pour in 2 cups of water. Set the trivet at the bottom of the stainless steel insert and carefully place the ramekins on top.
- Seal the lid and set the steam release handle to the "SEALING" position. Press the "MANUAL" button and set the timer for 15 minutes.
- When done, perform a quick release by moving the pressure valve to the "VENTING" position.
- Open the lid and carefully remove the ramekins from your instant pot.
- Cool to a room temperature without removing the aluminum foil.
- Calories - 309
- Fat - 27.3g
- Carbs - 2.3g
- Protein - 13.7g

STEAMED LEMON CAKE

Serving: 8
Preparation time: 10 minutes
Cooking time: 30 minutes
Ingredients:

- ½ cup all-purpose flour
- 1 ½ cups almond flour
- 3
- tablespoon
- white sugar
- 2 teaspoon baking powder
- ½ teaspoon xanthan gum
- ½ cup whipping cream
- ½ cup butter, melted
- 1 tablespoon juice, freshly squeezed
- Zest from one large lemon
- 2 eggs

Directions:

- Place a steamer in the Instant Pot and pour a cup of water.
- In a bowl, mix all the ingredients until well combined.
- Pour the batter into a dish that will fit inside the Instant Pot.
- Put aluminum foil on top.
- Place on the steamer and close the lid.
- Press the Manual button and adjust the cooking time for 30 minutes.
- Do natural pressure release.

Nutrition:

- Calories - 350
- Carbs - 11.1g
- Protein - 17.6 g
- Fat - 32.6g

POPPY SWEET PIE

Preparation time: 16 minutes
Cooking time: 6 hours
Serving: 6
Ingredients:

- 5 tablespoons poppy seeds
- 3 egg
- 1 cup cream cheese
- 1 cup flour
- 1 teaspoon baking soda
- 1 cup sugar
- 1 tablespoon orange juice
- 1 teaspoon butter
- 3 tablespoons heavy cream
- 1 pinch salt

Directions:

- Beat the eggs in a bowl. Add the cream cheese and continue to mix with a hand mixer. Then add the baking soda and sugar. Mix for 1 minute on the high speed.
- After this, add the orange juice, butter, and heavy cream. Sprinkle the mixture with the salt and mix until you get a smooth batter.
- Add the poppy seeds and stir the batter with a spoon. After this, cover the slow cooker lid with the parchment and pour the batter inside.
- Close the slow cooker lid and cook the poppy sweet pie for 6 hours on LOW. When the pie is cooked, chill it well and then remove it from the slow cooker bowl. Slice it and serve! Enjoy!

Nutrition:

- Calories - 395
- Fat - 22.9

- Carbs - 37.01
- Protein - 11

PEACH COMPOTE

Preparation time: 10 minutes
Cooking time: 1 hour and 30 minutes
Serving: 6
Ingredients:

- 4 tablespoons palm sugar
- 4 cups peaches, cored and roughly chopped
- 6 tablespoons natural apple juice
- 2 teaspoons lemon zest, grated

Directions:

- In your slow cooker, mix peaches with sugar, apple juice and lemon zest, stir, cover, cook on High for 1 hour and 30 minutes, divide into bowls and serve cold.
- Enjoy!

Nutrition:

- Calories - 182
- Fat - 2
- Carbs - 8
- Protein - 5

DARK CHOCOLATE CAKE

Serving: 6
Preparation time: 10 minutes
Cooking time: 20 minutes
Ingredients:

- 1 cup almond flour
- ..." cup Swerve
- ¼ cup unsweetened cocoa powder
- ¼ cup chopped walnuts
- 1 teaspoon baking powder
- 3 eggs
- 1 cup heavy whipping cream
- ¼ cup coconut oil
- nonstick cooking spray

Directions:

- Put the flour, Swerve, cocoa powder, walnuts, baking powder, eggs, cream, and coconut oil in a large bowl. Using a hand mixer on high speed, combine the ingredients until the mixture is well incorporated and looks fluffy. This step will keep the cake from being too dense.

- With the cooking spray, grease a heatproof pan, such as a 3-cup Bundt pan, that fits inside your Instant Pot. Pour the cake batter into the pan and cover with aluminum foil.
- Pour 2 cups of water into the inner cooking pot, then place a trivet in the pot. Place the pan on the trivet.
- Latch the lid. Select "Pressure Cook" or "MANUAL" and set pressure to high and cook for 20 minutes. After the time finishes, allow 10 minutes to naturally release the pressure. For any remaining pressure, just quick-release it. Carefully remove the pan and let it cool for 15 to 20 minutes. Invert the cake onto a plate. It can be served hot or at room temperature. Serve with a dollop of whipped cream, if desired.

Nutrition:

- Calories - 225
- Fat - 20.0g
- Protein - 5.0g
- Carbs - 4.0g
- Carbs - 2.0g
- Sugar - 0.0g

CHOCOLATE BROWNIES

Preparation + Cooking time: 55 minutes
Serving: 10-12
Ingredients:

- 6 tbsp unsalted butter
- 4 tbsp unsweetened cocoa powder
- ¾ cup all-purpose flour
- ¾ tbsp baking powder
- 1 cup sugar
- ¼ tsp salt
- 2 large eggs, beaten
- ¼ cup chopped walnuts
- 2 cups water

Directions:

- Preheat a small pan on the stove, add and melt the butter.
- Remove from the stove and add the cocoa powder, mix well.
- In a bowl, combine the flour, baking powder, sugar and salt.
- Add the eggs and walnuts, stir. Add the cocoa mix, stir.
- Grease a 7- to 8-inch baking pan and add the batter.
- Cover the pan tightly with aluminum foil.
- Pour the water into the Instant Pot and set a steam rack in the pot.
- Put the pan on the rack. Close and lock the lid.
- Select MANUAL and cook at HIGH pressure for 35 minutes.
- When the timer beeps, use a Natural Release for 10 minutes. Uncover the pot.
- Allow the brownies cool and serve.

FUDGE CAKE

Preparation time: 18 minutes
Cooking time: 5 hours
Serving: 6
Ingredients:

- 9 oz sugar
- 6 oz flour
- 4 oz cocoa powder
- 1 teaspoon baking soda
- 1 tablespoon vinegar
- 1/3 teaspoon salt
- 5 oz milk
- 3 tablespoons butter
- 1 teaspoon vanilla extract
- 6 oz chocolate chips
- 1 cup water, boiled

Directions:

- Combine the sugar, flour, cocoa powder, and baking soda in the bowl.
- Add vinegar and salt. Stir the dry mixture gently with a fork. Then add the milk and vanilla extract. Add butter. Use the hand blender to mix into a smooth batter.
- Cover the slow cooker bowl with parchment and pour the batter inside.
- Sprinkle the dough with the chocolate chips and boiled water. Do not stir the dough and close the lid. Cook the fudge cake for 5 hours on HIGH. Serve it warm. Enjoy!

Nutrition:

- Calories - 549
- Fat - 13.9
- Carbs - 98.19
- Protein - 8

BLUEBERRY COBBLER

Serving: 2
Ingredients:

- 1 cup blueberry pie filling
- 2 tablespoons almonds, chopped
- 3 ounces yellow cake mix
- 2 tablespoons melted butter
- Vanilla ice cream for serving

Directions:

- Spray a 2-quart slow cooker with non-stick spray
- Spoon the pie filling into the slow cooker and spread it out on the bottom.
- Sprinkle with almonds and cake mix, and then drizzle the butter over it.
- Cover, and cook for 3 hours until the top begins to golden brown in color.
- Serve hot with vanilla ice cream.

Nutrition:

- Calories - 449
- Fat - 14 g
- Carbs - 78 g
- Protein - 2 g

COCOA BALLS

Preparation time: 5 minutes
Cooking time: 4 hours
Serving: 8
Ingredients:

- 2 cups coconut flour
- 1 cup coconut sugar
- ¾ cup cocoa powder
- 1/2 teaspoon baking soda
- 2 tablespoons lemon juice
- 2 eggs, whisked
- 1 cup coconut milk
- ½ cup coconut oil, melted
- 2 teaspoons vanilla extract

Directions:

- In a bowl, combine all the ingredients except the coconut oil.
- Mix well.
- Add the coconut oil to your slow cooker then add the cookie mix. Spread the cookie mix in the pan, cover and cook on low for 4 hours. Take spoonful's of the mix and shape into balls and serve cold.

Nutrition:

- Calories - 333
- Fat - 23,5
- Carbs - 33,4
- Protein - 4,1

Printed in Great Britain
by Amazon